YOU ARE
BIGGER
THAN
ZILLOW®

SCOTT FUTA

Rhino Bee Publishing

Table of Contents

1

Clients are Like Jewels

Over the years I have heard just about every bit of slang used to describe the people that we real estate agents work with through the course of transacting real estate. A closing, a unit, a side, my client, mister seller, misses buyer, my folks, a listing, a buyer, a seller, a purchaser, tire kickers, lookie-loos, a sign call, a referral, a showing, and many others. None of these terms are ultra-flattering and some are a bit condescending but generally accepted as the norm. I am guessing that none of you had to pause to try to figure out who I was referring to with any of the above slang, right? The terms we have developed to identify the people we serve in our industry are common and in many ways nearly identical to the overall approach that too many of the agents in our profession provide. In a word, generic. No different from the service provided by a help desk, a 1-800 phone number to reach a call center, or a website. I remember a lesson taught to me decades ago by my stepdad, Dick. He ran his own video production company along with four partners. They called it Penta-vision, and it was started when the university where they all worked dissolved its in-house video production company. Dick was a very conservative man who proceeded cautiously when it came to business. In fact, I was actually surprised when my mother told me that Dick and a few of his colleagues had started the company. Starting his own company was not something that I ever would have thought he would do, given his cautious and conservative nature. Over the next many years, the five of them were extremely successful in securing new clients and earning repeat business and client referrals. Shortly after the launch of the company, Dick and I were talking about how much work it was to actually "earn" a client—not just the opportunity to "get" their business, but the labor of love that it is to earn their trust, respect, and referrals and all of the hard work it took to exceed the expectations of clients. Dick had a unique way of explaining what being of service to a client actually meant to him. He said, "Scott, having a client is like being entrusted with the safety and care of a priceless jewel."

I said, "Man, that's really good—"
Before I could say any more Dick said, "No, listen. They are like rare, precious, valuable jewels. Scott, picture a jewel wrapped in a leather pouch. It is my job to take the utmost care and protect it from harm. You always keep that jewel in a special place and care for it like it is the only one you have, the only one that exists. But then you notice that you have all these beautiful jewels, each one special and unique. All different sizes and shapes, all needing varying degrees of your attention to fulfill the duty you were entrusted with to care for them. That is what serving a client is."

I often remember the story Dick told. It always serves me well. I do think of that story now and again when I have to deal with a "difficult jewel." That story provides me with a clear perspective of how to approach those situations. Top agents know what is at stake. Top agents never lose sight of what their duties to the public and their clients are. Top agents are able to look past the frustrations of the moment and see the big picture.

A jewel and a client share three of the same qualities. They are precious, they are rare, and they are immensely valuable. First, a client is precious in that they *allow* top agents to serve them, giving purpose to the agent's talents and skills. It is like the chicken or the egg conundrum. An agent may be the most skilled and talented purveyor of real estate on the planet; however, without a client to serve, the agent's skills and talents are meaningless and have no useful purpose.

Second, clients are rare in that they allow you to engage with them from a position of trust. Trust is a rare thing for any person to lend to another, especially when someone lends us their trust based on a recommendation from someone they know, based on our marketing efforts, or based on reviews they read online. Never underestimate the rare gift of trust. Do not take it for granted, and never take it lightly.

And finally, matters of money do still matter, but not how you might think. Yes, it is clear that a client is valuable in a quantifiable sense, but those numbers are merely a sugar coating. I am not suggesting that the reason we are in business is *only* to serve others, never earn a dime, and live the financial life of a monk. Absolutely not. As you read along and take in all of the ideas and overall approach to the real estate business that I present, take it in through the lens that we are in business to make a profit, to make money and earn commissions. In fact we owe it to our clients and the people that we serve, because if we fail to earn a living in the real estate business, we will fail at our bigger purpose: to serve them. Commissions, compensation, money, earnings, and profit are a *result* of being in the real estate business. Serving people is the *purpose* of being in the real estate business.

The vast and endless value of a trusted client is far, far more than monetary. Clients allow agents the means to live a satisfying and wonderful life and live a life on their own terms and with a purpose bigger than themselves. As agents we get the privilege of earning a great living without being a slave to a time clock, without being tied to a desk, and without being under the constant supervision of a corporate boss. Although we must remain accountable, what a wonderful vocation we have chosen, or perhaps what a wonderful vocation that has chosen us. Either way, agents should never take for granted their purpose of serving others. That purpose gives them the ability to live and work in a unique way. Never take for granted the value of each and every client.

Right now in the realm of real estate sales, the traditional way that the business of real estate is conducted, standards are being called into question. Specifically some folks question the value of doing business the "analog" way by engaging the guidance and expertise of a real estate agent when selling or buying a home. Some people have the idea that technology provides a level of efficiency that can or should either limit or eliminate the need for the expert advice and guidance of a real estate agent. I completely disagree. However, before we examine all the quality guidance and quantifiable value that top real estate agents deliver to their clients, let's delve into the meat and potatoes, or eggplant and tomato sauce, if you prefer, of how real estate search platforms have evolved and are providing more and more real estate services and are disrupting the real estate industry.

2

Zillow.com, Realtor.com and Others Like Them

The buzzword in today's real estate industry as a whole, without a doubt, is *disruption*. Disruption is what Zillow.com, Realtor.com, Trulia.com, Homes.com, and many other real estate search platforms have caused. They have successfully disrupted the traditional way that a home buyer and a home seller access real estate information online. They did not create most of this information; they just collected it, organized it, built online platforms to display the information, and then sold leads and advertising back to the collective agent-body that actually took the listings in the first place. This process is commonly known as third-party aggregation of information. The sites collect information from public records in counties and municipalities all over the United States as well as collecting Internet Data Exchange, or IDX, information from local Multiple Listing Services, or MLS, as well as homeowners and their site's users and then display the information on the internet. Simple. Not diabolical or sinister, with intentions of taking over the world, I believe that they just intend to commoditize real estate transactions, that's all.

These platforms allow users to search the data on homes and rentals and allow them to look at, through MLS IDX connections, the pictures, descriptions, marketing, and videos that other agents paid to create. Again, simple.

Many of these platforms also sell advertising of various kinds to agents. These same agents are the ones who create the content in the form of video tours, professional photographs, property descriptions, and detailed and unique information about the properties for sale. When consumers visit these sites and enter their contact information or request to be contacted by an agent, this action in turn creates a buyer or seller lead. The companies that operate these platforms then sell the leads to real estate agents who pay for access, sometimes through a subscription. The leads are a revenue source. This model, in all shapes and variations, is in full force and expanding and evolving at a fast clip. There are growing voices within the real estate community that are unhappy with the way large technology companies are disrupting the industry. I am not one of them. In fact I welcome the disruption and the enormous opportunity it has created for real estate agents. Maybe it is the below-average real estate practitioners who are upset, scared, or worried or the part-time dabblers in real estate who are concerned. I cannot even guess. In my experience, top real estate agents love competition. Ultimately what the disruptors will create is an environment where only the fittest, most competent, and highly professional agents will thrive. The barrier to entry into the real estate industry has been very low for a long time, but this too will soon be disrupted. Only the strong, smart, professional real estate agents who chose to serve the public in the role of professional and trusted advisors will thrive.

Some of the technology companies in the market today have developed robust platforms and have done a great job laying out the existing market information that buyers and sellers and renters are looking for. They have made it easy to search the information in one place and have removed most geographical barriers to that end. As well, these technology companies spend millions and millions of dollars on national advertising campaigns promoting their individual sites. As a public service they have successfully done what real estate associations could not or would not do, and that is create and launch a national multiple listing service.

Most, if not all, of the technology companies and the platforms available, as they operate today, cannot serve "consumers" beyond either buying their house, as an iBuyer, or initiating a real estate transaction with one of their staff agents or an agent that partners with them. If you are not aware, the term *iBuyer* is relatively new to the industry and is an abbreviation of *Instant Buyer*. An instant buyer is a company, group, or entity that makes a cash offer to purchase a home, usually within twenty-four hours, to facilitate a quick sale or allow the seller to avoid going through the traditional process of listing, selling, and closing with a real estate agent. A consumer can get on any of dozens of sites and look at all of the homes in a neighborhood or look up a schedule of open houses, but there is not much that goes beyond facilitating the consumers' initial search. In a word, the interaction is transactional. A website cannot build a relationship beyond simple user engagement. The idea that the online home shopping experience will evolve into a click-and-buy home site with all the makings of an Amazon-type-platform for houses is a long stretch, in my opinion. The complexity of a real estate transaction will not go away just because of technological developments. Real estate transactions are complex by their very nature, and complex problem solving and conflict resolution requires a multitude of things to happen simultaneously, in order to reach a successful resolution. The typical real estate transaction comprises multiple multi-facetted negotiations that ultimately must result in the parties to the transaction coming to an agreement. The typical real estate transaction also requires someone to present the options, develop a strategy, and negotiate those agreements, in order to reach an outcome satisfactory to all parties. Many of the decisions that both buyers and sellers are faced with do not present either-or solutions and often require multiple layers of negotiation.

There are those who will argue that people will choose the path of least resistance and capitulate to a new norm of buying and selling without negotiating. I am highly skeptical.

I was talking with an old acquaintance who is a Silicon Valley insider. He had recently made a substantial investment in an iBuyer company, and he spoke passionately of the platform and about how real estate sales are going to be executed completely online without agents. When I am in situations like those, I tend to just listen objectively, because there is always something to learn, especially from someone who is so connected to the world of technology. After about an hour of listening to him, I was able to boil down his rationale to its essence and understand the concept that these investors and developers are betting on and the basis for the large investments they are making. Basically they believe that home sellers will give up a larger portion of the equity in their home to use an iBuyer. They believe that rather than paying less to a traditional real estate agent and making a higher return on their investment, sellers want to avoid (his words) the hassle of the old, tired real estate process with an agent.

Although I agree with the premise that a small percentage of sellers may prefer the option to trade more of their equity for the ease of selling immediately, I find it hard to believe that the majority of sellers are willing to leave $5,000, $10,000, $20,000 or more on the table to avoid a thirty- to ninety-day process that he perceived as a hassle.

When an agent does the math and shows a seller they get a substantially higher return on their investment by simply investing one to three months of their time by listing with a top traditional real estate agent, sellers clearly see the value. Yes, some sellers will opt for the speed the iBuyer model provides; however, a reasonable person will not likely walk away from that much money simply to avoid listing and selling their home with a traditional agent. Bottom line, the levels of service being offered to the public are being disrupted, and the question is this: "Can technology eliminate the traditional real estate agent?" Based on my experience and my countless interactions with clients and people of all different personality types over the course of hundreds of transactions, my answer is "Not likely."

Nimble in the Real Estate Marketplace

If you have been an agent for any length of time, I am confident that it is clear to you that the real estate market, generally speaking, always has and always will experience rapid, unpredictable change in abrupt and dynamic ways, nuanced by local and regional economic forces. And if you have been an agent for any length of time, you may also be able to relate to the "voodoo" moment when you can just *feel* that a change in market conditions is looming. For example, let's say that home sales in an area have fallen off a cliff, yet home prices in the MLS have not fallen. Or the average days a house spends on the market before the seller accepts a purchase offer has not increased, but you just feel it coming. As an agent at work daily in your market, you can read the subtle signals and feel the winds of change starting to blow.

When I see the subtle changes and I feel the market is shifting, I speak with Cheryl. She started selling real estate in the 1980s and has the battle stripes and market expertise to feel when the market is poised to shift. Usually I mention to her what I am seeing in the market and with clients' attitudes, and she usually agrees, if not immediately, within a short time. Cheryl would come to my office, stand in the doorway, and say something like, "You know, Scott, I think you might be right. Ever since we talked about the market shifting, I have been noticing (X, Y, or Z) too."

Sure enough, we as agents have our "circle of trust" comprising the lenders, contractors, fellow agents, title professionals, and inspectors we consult with. My colleagues also notice the sales activity turning up or ticking down, see the increase or decrease in buyer or seller enthusiasm, and feel the market shifting before it showed in the numbers. Just like a recession is usually months old before the low economic activity officially shows in the numbers, most real estate market information is comprised of lagging indicators. Considering that fact and that most of the real estate search platforms have cut their teeth in an ascending market, I will bet on the agility and nimbleness of agents to adapt to markets head and shoulders above any algorithm. There is extreme value, in the form of real dollars, in a top real estate agent's ability to sniff out which way the market is heading and developing strategies to get out in front of shifting markets. Being connected at a local level, even a hyper-local level, has enormous value to the clients we serve.

One of the advantages that top real estate agents have is that typically they live, work, and play each and every day in the community that makes up the market they serve. And they take that advantage for all that it has to offer. They attend city and town council meetings; they know who their state and local representatives are, and the best of the top agents actually talk to their representatives. They voice concerns, learn about upcoming legislation, and make requests. Imagine all the people who would love to be connected a bit more to local and state issues, but do not have the time, energy, or forethought to do so. I bet it is a lot of the people that already know you, like you, and trust you. Take a moment and realize the enormous opportunity this presents to you to serve the people of the community and your clients. The fact of the matter is that a website cannot compete with a top real estate agent at that level.

On a daily basis agents all over the country participate in activities within their communities and leverage their connection to the community to better serve the public and clients. If an agent is into fitness and health, for instance, they probably know of the best fitness trainers, gyms, and public trail systems in the area. Taking it a step further, if they are into the fitness lifestyle, they probably will know about any new fitness stores coming to the area or perhaps they have heard about a new CrossFit gym that will be opening. People find this information valuable, and this type of insider information is not important only to fitness types. Nearly everyone within a community will find value in knowing about new business openings, for example, and this information will surely be of interest to anyone who is vested in the community.

Your ability to gather and distribute information regarding the intangible assets within the community are also of great value. Have you ever stopped to think about how much people appreciate knowing things about their community that they were previously unaware of? That may sound a bit weird, but to put it simply, they don't know what they don't know. For example, is there a nice outdoor area where you walk your dog? Is there a restaurant you frequent that has seasonal outdoor seating or great happy-hour drink specials? People love to know this type of information, and top agents go out of their way to provide it.

Another valuable way that agents can keep people in the know and one that might directly affect local property values is the opening or closing of a company, government office, park, or restaurant. A large recreation project that is being proposed adjacent to a neighborhood, hypothetically speaking, may boost home prices. This is information agents must be aware of and share with their sphere of influence, past clients, or the general public. A website cannot operate this way.

Most iBuyer models require the home seller to give up a sizable portion of their equity for the convenience of a quick sale. How many people truly understand this fact? Real estate agents have the obligation to educate the public on the benefits and costs of selling a home using an iBuyer model. People will find value in knowing the basics of how various companies and platforms function and the costs associated with them. The idea that technology alone can remove the complexities from a real estate transaction must be clearly articulated and presented. Many leaders in the real estate industry today are doubling down on the idea that agents enabled by technology conduct business, communicate, and serve clients more efficiently and at a very high level. I cannot identify how technology will more efficiently handle buyer's remorse, which usually shows up about twenty-four hours after contracting on a home or how technology will negotiate a low appraisal, which requires give and take on both sides, or how technology will know the hot buttons in unique scenarios that top agents must find solutions to. Put simply, technology cannot.

The basic question comes down to this: Can a website or technology platform replace real estate agents? The facts do not support it. It is evident that technology has the potential to replace the weak agents, without a doubt. Top real estate agents, however, will always be in demand; however, the days of getting your license and jumping into business without the backing of a team or strong brokerage are coming to an end. Big names in the industry predict that the number of licensed real estate agents will shrink dramatically over the next decade, one predicting as much as a 40 to 50 percent drop in total agent count. Top agents know they have to regularly and artfully showcase their value. The fear is real, therefore, if you are a weak real estate agent. For top agents, it is time to control the controllables. It is time to showcase your value. It is time for you to serve your people at a level higher than ever before.

Let's get started learning how.

3

The Multiple Businesses
Real Estate Agents Are In

Okay, so you are on fire and ready to serve every person that you come in contact with. You are ready to provide the highest possible service and net your clients the most money the market will allow, but have you stopped and taken a mental picture of what such an endeavor will entail? Let's face facts. The real estate marketplace and the public that operates within it are woefully underserved. Sadly, this has been the case for…well, forever. It is sad that the public perception of real estate agents has us ranked near the bottom of every survey, usually somewhere above politicians, but about equal to used-car salespeople. The bad news is that the public definitely holds real estate agents collectively in low regard. The good news is that this low public perception presents a major opportunity to top agents with the willingness and drive to put in the hard work to blow the socks off of people in terms of their overall home buying or home selling experience. Because I am a glass-half-full kinda guy, I see this as a tremendous opportunity to be the *but*, as in "Some real estate agents I have dealt with in the past have been flakes, *but* we found a really great one. Our agent now, Jill…do you know Jill? Jill has represented us on the sale and purchase of our last three homes, and she also helped a few of our friends and my brother, who feel the same way we do about Jill. We love our real estate agent. We love Jill."

Cue the ticker tape parade!

If you have been around the business any length of time, I am sure you have heard at least a few of these type of testimonials about agents from their clients. I sure have. Do you think Jill's clients feel this way about her because she wrote a clean contract or negotiated like a master? There is no question that an agent must be great at conducting real estate transactions, but my guess (and it ain't no guess) is that Jill loves on them, takes care of them, provides them with great market information and the reasons why the information is important to them and consistently follows up and stays in touch. Without a doubt Jill has proven her loyalty to them and showcased her value way beyond the confines of a thirty- to forty-five-day real estate transaction. Without question, Jill performs the duties of a real estate professional on behalf of her clients with the utmost skill and care, but a connection like this one goes way deeper than Jill's merely being good or even great at what she does during the course of a real estate transaction. Jill's clients clearly are reciprocating the attention and admiration that they receive from her. That deep connection can start with a transaction, but it cannot be cemented in that short period of time. It must be earned. More on that subject later.

So what is the problem? Why aren't all agents serving their clients the way Jill serves her clients? The truth is that most real estate agents fall short, and we will talk about the three key drivers most real estate agents miss entirely when it comes to serving their clients and the public at large.

Most real estate agents reduce their real estate practice to a transaction-centric endeavor. There it is in a nutshell. An agent may provide impeccable service throughout a transaction. During the course of the sale, the agent's communication is second to none, in fact they might even receive praise for how tactfully they are at over-communicating. The agent "sets the field" in the client's mind, preparing them for situations that may come up, contingencies that may arise, or to help them brace for the shock of an unreasonable repair request from the buyers. Throughout the process, they provide their clients with all of the relevant information needed to make informed, fact-based decisions. They develop a strategy to negotiate for the most advantageous outcome for their clients and masterfully get their client to the closing table by accommodating their availability, perhaps even facilitating an offsite signing of the closing documents. The agents successfully execute closing, without delay or detour and then... crickets. Nothing. Nada, Zilch. Maybe the agent might call once after closing to make sure all is well or to handle a few post-closing details, but that is where the relationship ends. It is kind of like a really interesting one-night stand. Good for you? Good for me? Great; see you around. Sadly, many agents miss the opportunity to show their loyalty to their clients after such a great real estate experience. It is wasted potential. It also makes an agent look like they were just chasing a paycheck. We all know that any real estate agent who has been practicing real estate for more than a few years is not in it *just* for the money. There are many other easier ways to earn a living. The reality of earning a living as a real estate agent is always more than just a financial quest. In fact top agents know that the agents who *just* chase paydays usually do not last long in this business. Regardless of what we all know, perception is reality. Trust me, you never want the perception of a money-chasing one-night stander, even if it is clearly not the agent's intent, the mere perception is a killer.

Another big miss by real estate agents is when they reduce their entire value proposition to a discounted commission. Before I open this can of worms, I am in no way attempting to price fix, collude on commissions, or even suggest what *any* agent should charge. Whatever commission agents and their clients agree to is beside the point, 0 percent or 100 percent; it does not matter, and it does not come down to the amount. It comes down to your message, which is what real estate agents must understand. By advertising as a "discount" broker or agent, they are simply announcing "ANYONE CAN DO WHAT I DO. IN FACT I AM SO BAD AT MY JOB THAT I CAN COMPETE ONLY ON PRICE."

The type of agents who advertise this way are in a race with one another to the bottom, and at the bottom, no one wins. What does such a message really say about the agent? I will tell you what is says, "I AM NOT A MASTER NEGOTIATOR. IN FACT I AM TERRIBLE AT NEGOTIATING. MY MARKETING MESSAGE PROVES IT!"

Agents with that type of message essentially laid down on the starting line. If they are willing to sell out their own interest so quickly without making a case for themselves as a skilled agent in a desperate attempt to "get someone to use them as their agent," then what does it say about what lengths the "discount" agents will go to protect their client's best interest? I will tell you what is says: not much to reinforce the agent's skills of negotiation. I am not claiming there is no market for discount brokers, but their value is eroded when they choose to make their marketing message first and foremost all about their success fee.

Agents are terrible at communication. I am not referring to their communication throughout the course of a transaction. Most agents have that type of communication locked down tight as a drum. I can honestly say that over the many of years selling real estate, I have rarely run into a real estate agent who is a total communication loser. Some are stronger in this area than others; however, I am not talking about the urgent game-time communication that takes place during the course of completing a transaction. I am talking about long-term, loyalty-driven, value-added communication. Most real estate agents are like the bandwagon fans or fair-weather fans, which is what my grandma, Gee-mee, used to call them.

As an example, take a moment and think back to the 2016 baseball season. You might remember those lovable losers, the doormat of the national league, the Chicago Cubs and their World Series win. In 2016 the Cubs broke a seventy-one-year losing streak to win the National League pennant and broke a 108-year streak of not winning the World Series. Both were record droughts in Major League Baseball. I became a Cubs fan in 1992. I went to a game and immediately fell in love with the Cubs. I fell in love with the small, shitty ballpark, all the bars around that shitty stadium, like The Cubby Bear and Murphy's. Hell, the intersection of Clark and Addison was in the classic movie, *The Blues Brothers*.

As a side story, I met my wife, who was from Chicago, and things were getting serious, when the question was asked, "Cubs or Sox?" My father-in-law, Mike, grew up a couple of blocks from Wrigley Field. My mother-in-law, Maryalice, had season tickets for years. My wife and I named our second son Ryne (Cubs fans will understand), and back then my father-in-law almost exclusively drank Budweiser. So for long-time Cub fans, it was not hard to separate the tattered, dirty, and well-worn Cubs hats from the clean ones. You see, all of the sudden, a lot of people claimed they were Cubs fans for forever. Some guy even called my son, Ryne, a bandwagon fan. My son's response: "My name is Ryne."

The guy said, "Yeah, so what?"

My son then said, "And who is the bandwagon fan? Have you ever heard of Ryne Sandburg?"

Long-time Cubs fans were not upset with the droves of bandwagon fans that popped up overnight in October 2016, but we sure could spot them a mile away. My point in telling that story is to illustrate that you might appear to your clients to be a bandwagon fan, to be willing to show up only when times are good and there is something in it for you. Agents must showcase their loyalty when clients do not immediately need their services or when it is clear that they are not in the market to be selling a home any time soon. To overlook that type of communication is a critical mistake that can and will lead to the situation of driving by a past client's home only to see another agent's sign in the yard. Agents have to show their loyalty to their clients and stick with them through thick and thin. The very best way for agents to prove they are there for their clients in the past, present, and future, is to communicate that fact to them through action.

Another item that falls within the realm of communication is empathy. Top real estate agents always have empathy for the people they are entrusted with serving. Empathy is one of those words that everyone seems to recognize but cannot clearly define. Below is the Merriam-Webster definition. *EMPATHY: the action of understanding, being aware of, being sensitive to, and vicariously experiencing the feelings, thoughts, and experience of another.*

Most real estate agents are filled with empathy for their clients during the course of a transaction but totally forget about what their clients might feel after a transaction, when the great real estate agent they knew suddenly falls off the face of the earth. It is your duty to know your clients' basic wants, needs, goals, and desires when you take on the responsibility of serving them. If you do not know what your clients' basic motives and desires are, you need to find out. What a great reason to meet up with a past client for coffee or lunch some time! There are 365 days in the year. Pick one and schedule a time to meet with a client. Do this multiple times with all of your past clients. You will be shocked by what you can learn about someone over the course of a forty-five-minute lunch.

Once you get a glimpse into what drives and motivates your people, you will undoubtedly find an impactful way to guide and serve them with empathetic motives. For example, if you learned that they are huge hockey fans and you hear that someone is selling tickets to a playoff game, you might drop them a quick text to ask if they would like to buy them. It is pretty simple stuff, but I am telling you, communicating with empathetic motives will go a long way in serving people and earning their loyalty. If you do not believe me, try testing it out. You will be shocked at the response you get when you show a little interest in their wants, needs, desires, and goals.

Another example of empathetic motives on display is when during a home search clients share with you some of the must-haves of their next home, your obligation is to remind them of their stated "musts" if they start to stray from them. For instance, let's say you are helping clients who tell you that their next home must have a three-car garage. After a few days of seeing homes, your clients send you listings that happen to have two-car garages and ask for a showing. This scenario requires you to remind them of the initial conversation that you had. You might ask, "What has changed that you don't need a three-car garage?" Or maybe, "Mr. Buyer, do you remember telling me that one of the items your new home must have was a three-car garage?" Perhaps something has changed, and they have decided that the size of the garage is not as important as they thought it was, but it is your job to guide them with empathy. It is never an easy conversation to have, but they will appreciate your loyalty to their goals in this situation as well.

Let's also consider that Realtors® adhere to a code of ethics. Why do they agree to abide by these ethics? Why do Realtors® agree to take an ethics class every few years? Well, as a starting point, ethics, as defined by Merriam-Webster, "are the principles and/or conduct governing and individual or group." The reason for this, as I see it, is simply because temptation and human nature are often poor guides in situations that may pit an agent's interests against those of their clients. In moments of doubt, a code of ethics serves Realtors® as a standard guide or lens through which to view the situation and make an ethical decision. This is the very lens that people use when making tough decisions or judgment calls. Making judgment calls against a backdrop of a code of ethics will absolutely give you grounds to protect the public's trust in you as an ethical practitioner. Without trust, your guidance and advice will be brought to question, and in an industry with the reputation and perception as ours, no transaction is worth losing that trust. Once your public trust is eroded or lost, it is extremely difficult, and in some cases impossible, to regain. Most importantly, trust is an essential building block, and maybe even the cornerstone, of loyalty.

What does it mean to practice the profession of real estate? Again, consulting Merriam-Webster, the professional practice of real estate means "to perform or work at repeatedly so as to become proficient [at the business of real estate]." An agent does this by constantly pursuing mentoring and completing training, participating in activities, and gaining in-depth exposure to the business of advising and guiding clients in the process of purchasing and selling real property. Part of your job description is that you must make a concerted and constant effort to improve your skills, knowledge base, and expertise related to the activities of real estate, in order to serve your clients at a very high level.

Okay, let's talk about your role as a fiduciary. A fiduciary, or serving as a fiduciary, is defined by the Cambridge Dictionary as follows: "relating to the responsibilities to care for someone else's financial interests in a suitable way". Well, what position does this put you in with your clients? It puts you in a position to know your clients' motivating factors that will drive their decisions to purchase or sell. As a rule, top real estate agents never discuss the motivating factors of their clients unless doing so will bring the most benefit to their clients. They do this with only with the client's permission. Take a look at your agency agreements. Most of them have some language addressing this subject. Remember, running your mouth can cost your clients significant sums of money if you share the wrong information without permission. Now, on the flip side of the transaction, many cooperating agents do not understand this fact. And if you ask one magical question to the agents who are representing either the listing your clients are interested in or the buyers of your clients' home, they will share information with you, tons of information with you that may help you advise your clients. Here's the one magical, yet simple question: "What can you tell me about the house [or your buyers situation]?" That single question has yielded me tons of useful information that proved invaluable in guiding my clients through countless negotiations. A bit of advice: if you are asked this question, the most effective response is, "Well, tell me what you want to know." The main point to take away is that your clients, in a grounding of trust, share a lot of information with you. It is your professional position not to divulge privileged information without permission. In fact, it is your job to advise clients about what information they might not want to share, as long as doing so would not violate any laws or your code of ethics.

We have taken the first part of this chapter establishing the guidelines and parameters that agents operate within and the approach that top agents take to ensure successful and meaningful client engagement. Over the rest of this chapter, we will define and discuss the three businesses that top real estate agents engage in with clients each and every day.

We have established that the first order of business for all agents to master is that of the real estate transaction. I mean, that is insanely obvious, right? That is what agents do. Every day, agents take on the business of facilitating, negotiating, and successfully closing real estate transactions. This is what the public believes is the *single* job that all real estate agents do. The public sees agents completing the transactional activities of real estate, and that is what most people identify as what agents do. Okay, so then I will ask the chicken or the egg question. As an agent, did you show up on day one of your career in real estate with a robust database, with a fat book of business, and multiple transactions in various stages of the sales process? I am guessing the answer is no. I am sure that my experience was similar to many other fresh, new agents. Even if agents start their career with a team or with a mentor, they undoubtedly had to *first* get started with developing the other two businesses that top real estate agents operate. Even if an agent comes into the real estate business as an accomplished negotiator with a memory like a steel trap, completely competent in the entire transaction process and as a master in interpreting a purchase contract, without a client to serve, all those skills and talents are utterly and absolutely useless. Before an agent can serve a client, the agent *first* must find a client to serve.

Agents must be fully engaged in the business of initiating, building, and adding value to relationships. For lack of a better term, I call this *The Business of Serving People*. This is how agents will find their first clients, and eventually, why those past clients will seek you out to refer and conduct repeat business. The very basis of the real estate business must be recognized as that of serving people. The act of serving people starts way before the first closing, before contracting with a first client and getting them in the car to take them out and show houses, before taking the first listing, before everything else; you must *be* in the business of serving people. This is the business that you must first engage in, fully and completely, in order to *earn* the privilege to then work on a client's behalf. The business of serving people is, by far, the most overlooked element of success and the one that struggling new agents never seem to fully grasp. And to be clear, this is not simply time blocking and generating leads or holding open houses. The business of serving people is the business that drives the business, *comprende*? Do you get the picture? During my years and years of observing new agents, I've witnessed the same pattern play out with predictable frequency. As seasoned leaders in our broker-ages, we watch these new agents start their careers with their hearts on fire, only to give up and exit the business within the first two years. The National Association of Realtors® estimate that nearly 85 percent of all new agents leave the business within the first two years after licensing. Most of them are good, hard-working, and well-meaning agents who have the desire and skills to serve the public at a very high level. I think the high level of new agent washout is a sad waste of po-tential. I also think that the high washout rate is because no one has told many of these new agents that the business of fostering, building, and adding value to relationships is the most important business that they are in. In fact, it is the only business they are in. Again, think what came first, the chicken or the egg. To be successful, agents must show their loyalty to people simply through the act of serving them.

Building a business by serving others is not as sexy as the transaction side, nor does it provide the tangible financial rewards of successfully closing business. However, the secret is that setting out with the ultimate aim to accomplish nothing else but to serve others is infinitely more critical to an agent's initial success than any other endeavor.

Another critical business all real estate agents are in is the business of researching, studying, interpreting, understanding, and sharing information. Researching great and valuable information and then sharing and explaining its relevancy is at the core of the business of serving people. You need to know real estate information; community information; sales statistical information; macro and micro economic information; information on trends; local, state, and federal law information; and any other information that people, your people, the people you have chosen to serve, need to know. The business of being a source of information, more accurately, seeking out, understanding, and sharing information, is the number-one way that you will serve your people.

"Is the market up?"

"Is the market down?"

"What are they building on that vacant lot next to the supermarket?"

"What's going on with the new tax law in regard to the mortgage deduction?"

"Is now a good time to sell?"

"Is now a good time to buy?"

"Overall, how's the real estate market?"

"How much has my home appreciated since I bought it?"

"Should I sell my home or just rent it out and then buy another?"

These are the questions that are asked by my people. Now, when I say "my people," do you understand what I mean? I certainly do not mean just my clients, although they are my people. I also do not mean the people in my database or in my sphere of influence, but again those are my people too. What I mean is *anyone* I can serve. Some of my people have relatives in the real estate business and have never engaged or would never engage me as their agent; however, that is far from the best measurement to use to identify the people we will serve. The basic rule is that if there is an opportunity on any level to serve them, then they count as my people. Look first for the opportunity to serve, because without those opportunities, all the real estate skill, talent, knowledge, and abilities are useless.

The Real Estate Transaction Business

Take a minute and think about what it means to be in the real estate transaction business. Simply put, an agent is a salesperson providing a service, the service of advising and guiding clients through the process of buying and selling houses. Surprised? Blown away? Probably not. Top agents provide expert advice and opinions and protect their clients' financial position as a fiduciary. I personally do not take this responsibility lightly, but articulating what it means to facilitate a real estate transaction is pretty cut-and-dried.

Sadly, and to the detriment of their career in real estate, most agents focus only on the transactional piece of the real estate business. The commodity of facilitating a transaction comes in all shapes and sizes and with as many levels of competency as there are agents. Never take lightly your ability to serve your clients at a high level in the business of handling their real estate transactions, but the transaction itself cannot be the entire focus. Top real estate agents never lose sight of the fact that the transaction represents only about one-third of how they serve people.

The Real Estate Information Business

The information business requires an agent to be a student of real estate and all that it encompasses. Top real estate agents find joy and are deeply interested in studying, dissecting, and understanding real estate trends and cycles. Like a detective, top agents are always looking for clues that the market leaves monthly. Every MLS across the country gathers and regularly shares statistical information with its members, usually monthly, that tells the story of the current market. It is your responsibility to know the key points of the story that your local market is telling. I do understand that not all people pride themselves as a numbers person and that not everyone has a natural ability to interpret statistical data. But everybody can learn, and if you are in the business of real estate, you must learn. I am very fortunate to be a member of an MLS that does a tremendous job of scheduling and teaching classes on how to effectively use all of the tools that the MLS has to offer. I will bet that your MLS, or even your brokerage, has similar programs available to you. If you are in the unfortunate position of being a member of an association, MLS, or a brokerage that does not provide any training on where and how to gather information on your local market, try turning on your computer and seeking out videos online. The information is out there, and as I said, you must be a student of the business. You must pride yourself on knowing current relevant real estate information and be able to boil it down into digestible bits and share them and explain them to your people. After digging into the numbers and identifying a few interesting nuggets of relevant information to share, get in the habit of posting to social media or emailing a monthly news pieces to your people. In today's world, everybody has a cell phone, so video is another great way to share this information. More on affectively shooting and using video later.

You must realize that you are also tasked with the business of knowing current happenings and what is going on in your community. It is your business to remain up-to-date on the current events, activities, and general news relevant to your people within the community you serve. It can be as simple as finding the town's calendar of events and sharing it on social media. If there is a new restaurant or brewery opening up in your area, you could share the date and time of the grand opening. You will be surprised at how little effort it really takes to remain in the know and provide community information. There is an opportunity to get much more creative with elaborate video posts, monthly event reviews, organizing groups to attend an event or visit a new restaurant, or to meet with business owners and do a quick video promoting great new establishments. Perhaps you could create an opportunity by partnering with business owners by asking them to provide your people with an exclusive offer. The focus needs to be on consistently positioning yourself as the area expert who is in the know about all things within the community. As a point of being tactful, top agents know that they do not have to remind their clients about what they do every time they share information. Your people will know that you are a real estate agent by all of the great information that you share monthly about the local real estate market. Do not be a secret agent. Top agents find a balance and avoid leg humping them to death.

The Serving-People Business

What does this mean, the business of serving people? I have thrown around the term a lot, but what is the act of serving people, exactly? The idea of being in the business of serving people is simple. It means that you are in the business of providing more information, guidance, and expertise than you were are paid to provide. In the book *Think and Grow Rich*, Napoleon Hill lays out thirteen predictors of success that he identified through his research. One of those predictors of success is to "do more than you are paid for." Being in the business of serving people is rooted in Hill's concept of doing more for clients than you are paid for. I have taken it a step further and taken the approach to set out to serve my people with valuable and helpful information and guidance and to do and provide far more value than I am being paid for. Providing more value than you are paid to provide, or contracted to provide, or obligated to provide is an opportunity to prove up front that you are already loyal to the people you serve, before they ever are in need of an agent or an agent's services.

The Business of the Real Estate Transaction

When it comes to setting the tone and pace of a real estate transaction, top agents know that it is critical to identify and understand a client's wants, needs, and timeline. Believe it or not, many agents do not start with this basic premise in mind. Most of the average and below-average agents are so focused on "getting" the business of the buyer or "getting" the listing that there is no rhyme or reason to the approach they take. Top agents know that they must develop both a listing presentation and a buyer's presentation, practice it, commit it to memory, and present it the same way with each and every client, each and every time. During these presentations, top agents also know their client's success requires that the agent know how to ask great key questions and take good notes. Top real estate agents most often start with a pre-engagement questionnaire, whether it is for a buyer or a seller. In my years of selling real estate, I can accurately estimate that less than five out of one hundred agents even attempt to structure their business presentations with the end in mind. Furthermore, less than two out of one hundred agents will ever take the time to master it. Understanding the basis of a client's wants, needs, and timeline are the building blocks that drive the pricing strategy, the search criteria, and the marketing plan. Top agents know that without taking the time to gather and understand this critical information, they will be unable to take control of the process, effectively manage client expectations, and deliver the best possible experience and outcome to their clients. However, when these steps are taken up front, with all the parameters detailed, it is from that point that top agents develop listing strategies for their sellers and pinpoint exact search criteria for their buyers. I do not know how else an agent could go about providing world-class service and successful outcomes without the basic details firmly nailed down. It is within that framework that top agents know that they can procure the right selection of properties or accept a purchase contract from a buyer who can meet the client's timeline for closing. If an agent establishes these simple guideposts from the get-go, they can then effectively negotiate, communicate, advise, and close on behalf of their client's best interests.

The Business of Providing Information

Top agents are connectors. One of the many connections they are tasked with making is that of connecting people with relevant information. The valuable information that agents can provide to people is endless. All real estate is local. Agents must recognize this fact and firmly entrench themselves in the communities that they choose to serve. Agents who serve their people this way will position themselves as a source for information like, for instance, community events. Street festivals, farmer's markets, electronic or chemical collection points, spring yard waste collection programs, fall leaf collection schedules, block parties, holiday events—the available community information agents can provide to their people is literally endless. Luckily for top agents, most municipalities are not good at sharing this area-specific information or promoting these community events. The lack of clear communication that local governments or municipalities provide presents agents with endless opportunities to bring value to their people by taking on the role as the self-appointed source for sharing this information. As well, most municipalities publish information about upcoming construction projects or proposed building additions. This information is also available at town hall meetings or local government offices. This type of information is typically of high interest to the people in a community. New stores or restaurants, park expansions, or additions of trail systems are the types of information that your people will absolutely love to know. Everybody is curious, especially when it comes to what is going on in their community. To serve people at the highest level, top real estate agents know they must seize the opportunity to be known as a reliable source of community information. Agents who do this at even a basic level will find that after they have spent just a few months consistently providing this information, their phone will regularly ring with questions from their people asking, "What are they building on the lot next to the library?" Or "What store is going in over there next to the high school?"

You will literally be recognized as the area expert, and what better label to have as a top real estate agent!

To firmly position themselves in the role of expert connector and information source, agents also need to know and share information about good contractors, service providers, and business owners.

"That agent knows everybody!" The people I serve frequently say that about me and my team members. Trust is transferrable. Top agents make it a huge part of their business to get to know the good and identify the not-so-good service providers within their community. This will happen organically over time; however, top agents actively cultivate these relationships. Whenever you see or hear of someone who just had a project done, ask, "Who did this fine work?" Or "What is the name of the contractor you used?" Also ask, "Would you use them again?" People will tell you. It will be the most honest feedback you ever get. I tell the people I ask, "I'm always looking for great people for my people." Chances are pretty good that if your people liked working with them, they will sing their praises and will probably go out of their way to get you the contractor's business card. Chances are that if the person is happy with the service or work the contractor did, the person probably asked for a stack of cards. Many times all an agent has to do is ask about a new project or compliment some recent work, and it will open the door wide for an introduction. And, of course, if someone is less than satisfied, probe a bit and ask why. It is always great to know about those experiences as well. This endeavor is a labor of love. It is constant and ongoing. Top agents are constantly building new relationships with great service providers, nurturing those relationships, and culling the ones that either go out of business, retire, or fail to deliver top service to people. A reliable and well-nurtured professional network is also a source of great connections and referrals. When you do more than you are paid to do, you will eventually be paid for more than you do. Maintaining solid referral partner connections is one of the areas where you will watch that scenario materialize.

Lastly and most obvious is the business of market information. I have found that top agents must strike a balance in this area and deliver the Goldilocks level of valuable information to their people. Do you know what the Goldilocks level is? It is…just right! Top agents study, analyze, and clearly *understand* market trends and conditions as well as identify areas of opportunity and areas of concern. The key is to serve it up in digestible, bite-sized portions—not too much or too little; just right.

As real estate agents, we tend to speak our own language without much thought as to who actually understands it. I have found that between one and three key points is all I can effectively deliver to a person in one sitting. Top agents will find that delivering one or two pieces of easily understandable information goes much further than the old strategy of "show up and throw up". The method of sharing information by dumping gallons and gallons of facts, figures, and loads of data over people's heads is a major turnoff. Top agents strike a good balance between too much and too little when providing valuable market information. Remember, if your people are interested in learning more or have questions about the information that you share, they will reach out to you. This, after all, is the only reason that your knowledge and abilities are valuable; in the service of others.

The Business of Providing Predictable and Effective Communication

The people you serve, I am certain, live very busy and active lives. Whether their lives are filled with careers or kids or relationships or aging parents or even pets, people today live extremely full lives and do not have a ton of time they can afford to waste. And I'll venture a guess that when they do find unclaimed time, they do not want to spend every moment of it with you. That is not to say they do not adore and value you, but to put it another way, as far as communication goes, you are on their timeline; they are not on yours. The best approach to serve your people at an ultra-high level is to become predictable and effective. Face it; random, out of the blue, inconsistent contact is often missed. You have to put in the time and train your people to expect the communication they receive from you in a predictable timeline, in a predictable format, with predictable content. Not boring, but predictable. Top agents present information in a way that can best be described as being like clockwork. If agents send out a newsletter or market update on the second Tuesday of every month, their people will come to expect it at that time. After more than a year of sending out a monthly video newsletter, I had a production delay and the video did not go out at the scheduled time. We received no less than a dozen calls and emails asking why it had not gone out, if we had quit producing it, or if they had been mistakenly unsubscribed from our email list. Top agents train their people by being predictable, especially when it comes to making contact with them. As important as building and following a predictable schedule is that the schedule means nothing without delivering clear, concise, and overall effective communication. Information and messaging are absolutely useless if your people cannot relate to it. It is also important to remember the business adage, "People do not care how much you know until they know how much you care." There is no substitute for timely, clear, concise, and well-prepared communication. Top agents know this fact and put this type of communication in front of people like clockwork.

The Greatest of These Is Serving People

All right, it is fair to surmise that we would not be discussing any of these items if it were a waste of time. All three of the businesses that top real estate agents engage in are all clearly important, for the reasons that we have covered throughout this chapter. But what makes serving people the most critical? I can sum it up in a word: Proof. By choosing to build a business grounded in serving people, top agents *prove* to their people that they are absolutely loyal to their best interests. Over time, and especially after closing business, continuing to build a business rooted in serving people proves that you are a top agent who is committed and loyal to them as a valued and deserving human being. In the world today, people find themselves very accessible by the outside world through the wonders of social media, but the ease of using social media platforms has led to the lack of commitment to staying in touch. The net result is a growing group of agents who woefully underserve their people beyond the basics of the real estate transaction itself. If you make the business of real estate nothing more than transactional, people will make nothing more than a transactional relationship with you. Top agents actually seek out opportunities to serve, which clearly demonstrates that to top agents, people are a priority, a top priority. Top agents understand that it is not about the commissions they earn and it is not about any sales awards or recognition. It is entirely about serving people.

There are very few ways for agents to illustrate their true intensions, depth of character, and purpose for being in business. Many agents cover their websites in script font, laying out their commitment to "integrity, honesty, and experience" yet they have literally not spoken or communicated with some of their most cherished people in years. I attribute this behavior to an agent's lack of organization more than any ill intention. But who cares why it happens? Fancy, well-researched words and smartly designed marketing materials mean nothing if people do not believe that you are sincere. Top agents know that the best way to ensure that clients will be loyal to you is to demonstrate loyalty to them first.

It is important to make a clear distinction between providing people with a service and serving people. The distinction is simple. Providing people with a service is nothing more than a commodity, while serving people is an artform. Take a minute to think about most services you engage with. I am sure that you will discover that most are transactional in nature, and transaction coordination is impersonal, algorithmic, and regimented. When was the last time you went through a McDonald's drive-through? Did you actually feel served, or was it more like you were serviced? Was the interaction personal or more like a NASCAR pit stop? Compare that experience with the last time you dined at a five-star restaurant. The examples are all around us, drawing a clear distinction between serving people and providing a service. Serving others is relational and unique to the individual. Truly serving others is crafted through the use of vision, purpose, and understanding, all directed to serve the very personal and unique wants and needs of a person. Folks, that is a form of art!

4

Who is Supposed to be Loyal to Whom?

Agents should treat everyone as if they are already clients. Top agents understand this idea better than all other ideas when it comes to serving the public. Top agents understand that everyone they come in contact with will need their expertise one day in the future, or at the very least they know that people they come in contact with will know someone who will. One of the greatest mentors in the real estate game, Gary Keller, says that very simply, your success in the real estate business will come down to how many people think of you when they think of real estate. Since it is said that you never get a second chance to make a great first impression, you are auditioning for the privilege to serve new people every single day. When top agents are at the gym, their child or niece or nephew's school function, an event, or even at the grocery store—virtually every day and everywhere— they understand that they are auditioning. How they dress, how they carry themselves, the language they use, everything they do, in almost every case, is done in the presence of potential clients. No pressure, right? Do not fall down before you even leave the starting line.

Remember this too: even if agents never have had the opportunity to close a sale with a given individual yet, they still have the expertise that they themselves, or someone they know, will need one day in the future. To break it down to the simplest of terms, the only real qualification that one has to be a client is the need to be served. It is a pretty broad brush that we are painting with here, which is a good thing. Top agents are always on the lookout for people to serve. Still far too many agents have too narrow of a focus and are interested only in seeking out people with an immediate real estate sales need. That mindset represents pure transactional thinking, and agents who think that way will not get far. They are the agents who seem only to be chasing a commission. I am here to tell you that approach is a self-defeating way of thinking, not to mention the fastest way to becoming burned out with the real estate business. As an agent, especially one just starting out, there is a balance between being able to survive and make a living and playing the long game and maintaining the long-term focus on serving clients. Top agents never lose sight of the bigger picture.

Ponder this thought: when in the client relationship cycle are real estate agents paid? Are they paid in the beginning of a relationship cycle, in the middle of that relationship cycle, or at the end of the relationship cycle? Agents who work merely for a commission check might believe their compensation is earned at the end of the relationship cycle. Top real estate agents know, however, that their commission derives from a combination of all three. It is ultimately a matter of perspective. Remember, clients give purpose and value to an agent's skills, knowledge, and talents. From that perspective, agents are paid in the beginning of the cycle because, after all, without a client to serve, all of the skill, knowledge, and talent means nothing. At some point you are also paid your success fee, typically at a closing. Top agents correctly see a closing as the middle of the client relationship cycle. When agents successfully facilitate closing for a client, they are at the highest point of the relationship, because the agents just proved to their client that they have the right stuff. This is where average agents stop, or at the very least, pause the relationship cycle. Top agents know this is just the beginning, the second beginning, and that the relationship cycle never ends. This is the agent's opportunity to earn a client's referrals and ultimately the gold standard reward of a client's repeat business. It is critical that agents understand that they must keep working to earn those referrals and repeat business.

Agents, Be Loyal to Thy Client

One of my biggest pet peeves is when I hear an agent say something like, "I can't believe it! *My clients* listed with so-and-so agent. I took such great care of them five or six years ago. How could they do this to me?"

I always wonder, well, what have you done for this client lately that you earned the privilege to call them *"my clients?"* Have you stayed in touch with this client? Have you kept this client informed? The client is not at fault in any way, shape, or form for choosing another agent instead of a past agent. Their sense of entitlement is baffling to me. Somehow those agents believe that the client is responsible for thinking about them. They totally miss the point that it is the agent's duty to stay in touch with the client. In this scenario, the client did nothing wrong; in fact, the client did not "do" anything, because after the closing, neither did the agent.

The National Association of Realtors® conducts many studies researching habits of buyers and sellers. The information gleaned from these studies is fascinating. From the results top agents gain a lot of insight into the mindset of their clients and the public at large. One study of particular interest to me contains questions asked of people who recently closed on the sale of their property listed by a Realtor®. One of the questions is something like, "Did you list with the same agent who helped you purchase the home originally?"

Stunningly, only 12 percent of the time the answer to this question is "Yes."

If the answer is "No," then the client is asked, "Were you happy with your previous agent who helped you with your initial purchase, and if given the chance, would you have used that agent to list the home you just sold?"

A whopping 84 percent of the respondents answered "Yes." My gosh! Why, after all the hard work and after providing such a high level of service, do so many agents think it is the client's responsibility to keep in contact with their agent? It is up to the agent to build the relationship, and top agents know they owe their loyalty to their client, not the reverse. News flash: your clients owe you nothing, even if you did a great job for them the last time around. It is shocking to me how many clients actually do stay loyal to agents who have abandoned them. If you have spent any time prospecting and lead generating, chances are you have come across a few people who remain fiercely loyal to their last agent, even if the agent has not spoken with them in months or years.

The National Association of Realtors® statistics are really a silver lining, not a gray cloud. Are you ready to hear a huge secret that I am going to reveal to you in this book? Ready? TOP AGENTS STAY IN TOUCH WITH THEIR CLIENTS! Mic drop.

Okay, all sarcasm aside, it is obvious that staying in touch with your clients is worth every bit of effort that you put toward that endeavor, but many agents just plain fail at it. Top real estate agents take client follow-up much further. Top agents approach past client relationships with a nurturing mindset of building a foundation of loyalty *to* their clients, not *from* their clients. We have already established that an agent's skills, talents, and knowledge mean nothing without a client to serve, so clients are vital to your existence as a top agent. But take it a step further. Think of your clients as jewels that you need to protect. After all, we work with other real estate agents nearly every day, so we do run across our fair share of not-so-great practitioners. Top agents make it part of their mission to protect their clients from people in this business that suck. Yes, I said it, there are people in this business that suck at what they do—the exception surely and not the norm—however, they do exist, and our clients must be protected from them. So put on your red cape and start saving the day, every day, because top agents are in the business of serving people. Remember that *a service* is generally a transactional function with a defined end, and *serving* is a relational function and is ongoing. Throughout your career you will provide clients with many service-based functions; however, serving people is your primary function.

I am sure that the thought has crossed your mind that if serving clients is your main goal, when do you focus on earning a living? Great question. It is all about which perspective you choose to see it from. Top agents absolutely understand that *earning* is a direct result of *serving*, not the other way around. Earning a client results in earning a commission, and top agents know that a commission is a byproduct of great service. When agents choose to focus on the right daily activities, the results will come. When you choose to serve clients this way, you will be rewarded beyond your wildest dreams.

What more do you have to give others than to serve them? That is to say, what is your product? The reality is that serving others is your only product, and it is all you have got to give. In looking for opportunities to serve others, you will ultimately serve yourself. First of all, you will be much happier and more fulfilled by approaching the real estate business this way. As well, top real estate agents know that the real estate sales business is full of potential burnout. If you focus on serving others rather than chasing closings, you will be focusing on what really matters.

So far we have spent some time examining what agents have to offer their clients, the public, and other people by serving them. We have looked at what it means to have a servant's heart at all points before, during, and after a real estate closing. We have discussed some of the approaches and methods that top agents use in order to go out of their way to serve others, even before they become a client, let alone before they actually need anything from the agent. Coming from a point of contribution will pay dividends to you and those around you. At this point it is only fair to talk about some of the many other byproducts that you will experience as a result of serving others and showing them your loyalty early and often.

The people that you serve will go out of their way to talk about you and all the great things that you do for them. In talking about you and all the great ways you provide value to people, they will recommend you to others. They may refer business to you, yes, but the true measure is whether they also refer people to you. Will they want others to "get in on" all of the great information that you share about service providers, contractors, community events, construction projects, as well as real estate market information and community news? Over time and by building agent-to-client relationships built on loyalty and service, people will look to you for consultation on home improvement projects and your advice on the best areas to spend money on home improvements, in order to add value to their homes. And ultimately, people will love and respect you because you show that you love and respect them.

Another example of what you will surely receive from all your efforts is that people will recognize the benefit from their relationship with you far, far beyond money. It is true that "the bottom line" matters to most folks, but in building relationships based on your loyalty and through serving, people will not reduce you to merely just a cost. The value-add model is really lost in today's world, especially in our industry, where discounts are peddled about randomly on postcards and door hangers, promising some ultra-low teaser rate that turns out to be mostly smoke and mirrors.

When your approach is that of serving others and showing your loyalty to them first and in big ways, people will be willing to "show up" for you.

If you have watched any television programming during the Christmas holidays, you have probably watched *It's A Wonderful Life*. The story is about a small-town guy who had big dreams of getting out of his small town of Bedford Falls and making a big difference in the world. Through several turns of events George Bailey ends up having to forego his dreams of life in the big city to run his family business, Bailey Savings and Loan. Over the years George truly serves the people of his community. He does business with the people who need the loans the most and is instrumental in helping countless families realize the American dream of owning their own home. People turn to Bailey Savings and Loan when there is no other place to turn for a mortgage, particularly when Mr. Potter, the hard-lined, ruthless banker in Bedford Falls is not willing to help. Mr. Potter is best described as a warped, frustrated old man who personifies all of the qualities of a

Scrooge. One day a large sum of money goes missing when George's absent-minded Uncle Billy mixes it up in a newspaper that ends up in Mr. Potter's possession. Potter discovers the deposit slip along with money but does not tell anyone in hopes that Bailey Savings and Loan would be forced into bankruptcy because of the error, eliminating his only banking competition in town. After a long and frantic search for the money, George is on the brink of ending it all by jumping off a bridge. That is when he meets Clarence, his guardian angel, who shows him what life in Bedford Falls would be like had George never existed. Through cynical eyes, George slowly realizes the impact that he has had on many aspects of daily life and all of the good he has done for the people in his small town. George is given the gift of seeing how things could be so horribly different if he was not there to *serve* the members of his community. In the end George chooses to go back to his life as it was and face the consequences of the federal bank inspectors. When all the townspeople show up to donate their money to save him and rectify the lost money, it is only then that George truly realizes the divine value in serving others.

The town showed up for George Bailey in his time of need, not because they had to, but because George had unknowingly spent a lifetime showing up and serving others by always being loyal to their needs. The old black-and-white movie clearly illustrates what serving others will bring your way as well, if you are willing to selflessly serve others. It cannot be faked; it does not come cheap, and it takes time, but a life dedicated to serving others is a solid foundation of a life worth living.

Showing gratitude is a key ingredient in living a full life, and top agents know that following up and staying in touch with clients is the ultimate sign of gratitude. It shows clients—no, better yet, it *proves* to them that you will not forget them, that your intensions do not stop at the closing table. It is the proof to clients that you are a loyal and valuable servant, a servant that they need.

Okay, by now you can clearly see the logic and sensibility in proper follow-up with your clients, but let's dig a bit deeper and explore what proper follow-up and consistent contact really proves when it comes to reinforcing your display of loyalty.

Consistent, proper follow-up shows your clients that if nothing else, you are organized and disciplined. The trait of consistency by itself shows your clients that you conduct yourself in a very professional manner and that you manage yourself and your relationships in a caring and thoughtful way. It shows class and poise in a world often lacking those qualities.

Proper and consistent follow-up also illustrates your willingness to serve the people you are entrusted with serving without any sort of ulterior motives or strings attached. After all, you were already paid for services rendered, so your professional follow-up shows that you will remain there, now and forever, to serve.

Following up with clients in a regularly scheduled fashion also allows you to show off your creativity. Top agents know that communicating with clients cannot forever remain the tired same-old-same-old. You have to think outside the box to figure out ways to effectively communicate relevant and timely information that will add value to client's lives. There are only so many ways to remind clients that you are, in fact, a top-producing real estate agent. Top agents go beyond the basic script of repeatedly asking clients who they might know who is looking to buy, sell, or invest in real estate. It takes pure creativity to come up with offerings of value. And do not forget that there are really no new ideas, so do not be afraid to borrow any great ideas you see or experience. Top agents are always on the lookout for great marketing messages to borrow and adapt to make them their own. Just remember never to cross the line and steal copyrighted materials. There is a pretty clear line between adapting a great marketing message to make it your own and completely copying someone else's work. One area that is easily overlooked is the use of copyrighted music in your video content. Do not lose sight of proper sourcing and crediting, as well as purchasing the right to use music that you might edit and use in a video. There are literally dozens and dozens of sites on the internet that offer low-cost music as well as free sound tracks too. The bottom-line message is to keep everything you do ethical and on the up-and-up.

Proper follow-up will also remind clients that they did business with a top professional in the real estate field. Along with reminding them that you are a consummate professional, consistent and timely follow-up allows you to provide your client's with items and information of value. One idea that I think I invented was the flyswatter mailer. I sent out an envelope containing a house-shaped flyswatter branded with my logo and a little note attached that read Something Bugging You About Your House? Gimme a Call!

The note thanked them for being such great clients, wished them a great summer, and reminded them of how to get a hold of me. My team was bombarded with texts and pictures of the flyswatters in use. The flyswatter mailer is just a quick example of how you can use your creativity and a useful piece of plastic to stay in touch with your clients.

Another useful function of proper and timely follow-up is the opportunity to showcase recent accomplishments illustrating an agent's top-notch abilities. I like to call this type of correspondence *proof of performance.* It is used to highlight a top agent's sales performance, such as when the agent closes a real estate sale or helps people in a creative or special way. This type of follow-up can accomplish a few things. It can remind clients that you have solutions for problems that might be in the back of their mind. For instance, if you have a great granite guy or painter who helped one of your clients in the past, share a quick story of how your recommendation of a trusted vendor helped clients improve a property issue and sell their home faster or for more money. A story like this one may be the spark that helps a client who hates her countertops or has a few rooms ready for a new coat of paint get into action, even if the client only intends to repair or upgrade a home and not sell. Stories like these make it crystal clear that you help clients in many more ways than just by selling houses. Sharing proof of performance also reminds clients that you are, in fact, an expert who sell houses and that you are very, very good at it.

Top agents also use follow-up opportunities to highlight their vision and values. Whether it is an invitation to a self-defense class from an agent who practices martial arts or an offer to get involved in a community project that is near and dear to an agent's heart, sharing information and opportunities that are directly connected to an agent's own vision and values allows top agents to showcase their interests. It also offers proof that you are in business for something bigger that yourself.

Showing loyalty to clients by staying in touch with them offers you the opportunity to give without expectation of receiving anything in return. It is a way to prove to clients that you are with them for the long haul. Showing them that they matter to you is proof that you will not forget who they are. Ultimately it is tangible proof that your value goes far beyond the closing table.

Top agents also understand that they must remain consistent in their follow-up. If communication is filled with constant gaps, starts, stops, and long pauses, it gives the appearance of being completely unorganized. On the flip side of the coin, if there has been a long break in communication with your clients, you definitely are not doomed to lose them forever. If it has been awhile, even a long while, since you last made contact with a client, it is okay. One approach to get back on track with clients is to make a quick phone call to check in with them. This type of phone call will go a long way, especially if it has been a number of months or years since you last talked with them. A quick phone call might begin with a script like, "Hey, John, I wanted to call and apologize for letting so much time go by since we last talked. How are things going?"

Some agents might be reluctant to make a phone call like this one and may want to just send a card or mailer, rather than admitting that they dropped the ball on staying in touch. I say, "Feel the fear and make the call anyway." Think of it, if clients start receiving passive correspondence from you out of the blue, such as cards in the mail or random emails, it may come off as insincere and suspect, especially if they may have forgotten about you. Secondly, life moves fast, and they may have already sold their home using another agent. I have seen it happen. Spare yourself the embarrassment of appearing clueless to the new owner, not to mention wasting time and money sending mail to a stranger and make the phone call. A quick, sincere apology for letting so much time go by will serve everyone well. A phone call will quickly rekindle the relationship and get you back on track with your client. Never forget that consistency in communication with clients will further build and reinforce the trust that you have already built with them. After months and years of consistent follow-up, your clients will come to expect to hear from you. By creating an expectation, you create a regular and consistent opportunity of meeting expectations, which is really powerful, if you take a moment to think about it. By creating an expectation, you are meeting an expectation that you created. Whoa! Heavy!

You will be frustrated at some point by a client who never seems to engage. It is okay if some clients do not seem to value what you do for them with your follow-up. It is okay if some of your clients seem to ignore the follow-up that you provide to them. Top real estate agents know that the world is filled with different personality types. Keep in mind that different personality types respond differently. Instinctually, as people who care about our clients, our first reaction might be that we are not providing enough value or that we are irritating or upsetting people. Well, that is just not true. And furthermore, do not go projecting your thoughts onto other people. Case in point: once upon a time I received an internet lead. The person had searched and then viewed a single home valued at $1.2 million, which at the time was roughly three times our area sales average. My team followed up and followed up and followed up again and again. Crickets. No response. After many months, the agent I assigned to follow up with this person came into my office and asked, "Should I keep sending listings and things and corresponding with this person?"

Keep in mind that at this point this agent did not even know if she was corresponding with a man or woman, that is why she said, "this person."

I asked, "Has the person asked you to stop?"

She replied, "No."

I said, "Then keep sending relevant property matches until the person tells you to stop."

Do you know what happened next? That's right. Nothing ever came of it. The end. No, I am kidding. Actually the agent continued to stay in touch for nearly two full years. She kept sending emails of property matches and the person kept opening them (through our system we could track if the emails were being read). No other response; the person just kept opening the listing emails, until one day our agent received an email. It said something to the effect of "I will be in town next week, and I want to see these three properties. Do you have time to show them to me?"

It happened to be a guy relocating from the Southwest who was also a custom-home builder. Long story short, he bought a mid-seven-figure home and started looking for land to develop. While chatting after the closing, James mentioned that he had received correspondance from a dozen agents leading up to his visit to see those three houses. Out of curiosity, the agent asked James why he chose her as his agent. He immediately gave a simple reply, "Because you stayed in touch."

What is the moral of the story? You can never guess what a person is thinking, and if you try, you'll likely be dead wrong.

The above story often raises the question of how long an agent should go those extra miles to connect with someone. I will say it this way: either as long as it takes or until someone tells you to stop contacting him or her. It's pretty simple but also counterintuitive. Face it, when people digitally ignore you, it can be hard to keep the faith enough to believe that they actually appreciate your efforts. Keep making the effort until you make the connection, or until they clearly ask (or tell) you to back off. It is worth mentioning that if clients unsubscribe from your email list, are on the Do Not Call registry, or communicate in any way that they want to be left alone, respect their wishes.

5

The Language We All Speak and Understand

I think we have all heard the adage, or at least a version of it, that you never get a second chance to make a first impression. This is true, but vague. Long ago Skipper Pierson, an old Navy man and my first real boss in the working world, told me that you never get a second chance to make a good first impression. Since then I have adapted it to this: YOU NEVER GET A SECOND CHANCE TO MAKE A GREAT FIRST IMPRESSION. I am positive that most people understand this basic concept. People also understand that most often, the first memory people associate with you will likely remain with them and be connected to their perception of you. But let's look at that concept a bit deeper. Not only will a first impression last long into the future when forging a relationship, but a first impression will become your personal **brand**. Why are first impressions ultra-important in the world of top real estate agents? Mainly that first impressions are very hard, in fact nearly impossible, to change, because they are usually impossible to forget. The first impression you make is anchored to you and is the first thing that people attach to you as your persona. Were you seen as the well-dressed, articulate, well-spoken professional or as the belligerent drunk? Did you show up as the confident but laid back, approachable, friendly adult or the ball-cap backwards, faded T-shirt, flip-flop-wearing loudmouth who incessantly cussed? Top agents understand that they are always auditioning for new relationships wherever they go and that how you show up the first time is how you'll be remembered, always. I have heard all of the arguments made by all agents for all of the reasons. Arguments such as, "People should accept me for who I am and not judge me because of how I am dressed." Or another favorite of mine, "I dress like my target clients, because I want to make them feel comfortable." Or yet another, "My clients swear in front of me, so I am pretty sure it will not bother them if I swear too." Or another, "I just started as a real estate agent, so no one expects me to have my business cards yet."

I am not here to argue the validity of any of these reasons, excuses, or explanations. I am not here to listen to someone preach about the virtues of not judging a book by its cover or that people should be solely judged by the content of their character and nothing else. Hey, I agree. *But* human nature is much different from the politically correct flavor of the week. All I am saying is that if we acknowledge that people do, and always will, judge other people by their first impressions, why not take a few steps to control of the things that are controllable? After all, first impressions completely set the foundation for the relationship that you will build with someone. So why not make sure that you put your best foot forward and make the foundation solid with a positive first impression?

A good example to provide you with food for thought are television commercials that feature doctors or scientists. How are they presented to the public? Take a moment and think about what comes to your mind. White lab coats, holding clipboards, usually wearing glasses, chin held high showing confidence, and doctors usually wear a stethoscope around their neck and scientists stand near lab equipment. Why do corporate advertisers painstakingly position such characters in commercials for pharmaceuticals, over-the-counter remedies, complex chemical-based products, and so forth? For one reason: to illustrate credibility. The implied message goes something like, "Not only do we say X about our product, but highly educated and skilled authorities do too."

What kind of confidence would someone have in a pharmaceutical product endorsed by a flip-flop-wearing teen-ager that professed, "This stuff works like a charm, man."

Never forget that first impressions are the lens that others will see you through for a long time to come. Take great care in managing your personal brand when it comes to making a great first impression.

To be clear, I am certainly not advocating that a person be fake or less than genuine. If you are the kind of person who feels the most comfortable in blue jeans and T-shirt, that is just fine; however, it would not kill you to step up your wardrobe a notch and wear some casual khaki slacks and a nice collared shirt with your brokerage logo on it.

Everyone Appreciates the Truth

Being truthful is a character trait that without a doubt everyone appreciates, especially when it is coming from their real estate agent who is representing them in a fiduciary role. In the case of truth telling, an agent's bedside manner will make all of the difference between a client feeling informed or insulted. It can totally backfire when attempting to present the truth creatively. These are the cases when people feel insulted. Agents usually try a creative approach when they are attempting to deliver bad news to their clients. The best approach is to be direct and on point and avoid mincing words. That is not to say that everyone will love the truth you are sharing, and it is not out of the realm of possibility that they may even react strongly to the truth. But people crave the company of truth-tellers. Proper bedside manner in presenting the truth is an absolute art form and must be carried out with the specific audience in mind; however, avoid telling half-truths, little lies, or sugar-coated truths. Top agents know that respect is earned and that a primary way that an agent earns respect is by telling the truth. An element to consider when counting the costs of telling half-truths and sharing sugar-coated facts is that this approach will train those you come in contact with to second guess almost everything you tell them. Whether you are dealing with a client, an inspector, or another agent, being unquestionably truthful, no matter how uncomfortable it may be, is the only way to approach things. In a business relationship, being labeled as a liar means certain death to your credibility, because information that is perceived, or in fact is, anything less than the truth appears as an attempt to deceive. Deceptions are lies, and if you give the impression that you are a liar, changing that impression is nearly impossible.

After all, the truth is nothing more than facts, and everyone appreciates facts, especially when making big decisions.

The Facts and Fact-Based Decisions

Think of your last major purchase. Perhaps it was a computer, car, bicycle, phone, gym membership, appliance, home-study course, training program, or maybe something else. Regardless what it was, if you spent a few hundred dollars or more, you probably did not grab the first thing you came across. Such a purchase requires some research. Most thoughtful people take time to find and compare facts. Why take the time? Simply put, most adults understand that fact-based decisions are much more reliable than emotional or impulsive decisions. In the absence of facts, people are left to make decisions based on emotion, impulse, or a SWAG (scientific wild-ass guess).

Have you ever made a major purchase purely based on emotion? What was the outcome? In my experience, any time I have made such a buying decision I have always had some feelings of regret or remorse. Usually high-dollar knee-jerk purchase decisions do not turn out well. When making impulse buys, I have a tendency to overspend or later I find out I could have gotten more features in a similar product from a different manufacturer, if I had taken some time to shop around. It may not always go terribly wrong, but it often seems there was a better choice available that I did not take the time to discover or even consider. The reality is that facts are rooted in truth, and all people appreciate facts and the truth, both as they relate to making decisions and dealing with a trusted professional advisor.

An Offer of Honesty

As I mentioned earlier in this chapter, professional bedside manners can have a huge impact when presenting the truth to your clients and people in general. So if you find yourself in a situation where you have to share less-than-exciting information with your clients, and you absolutely will, there are a few things to consider before dropping a thermonuclear truth bomb. The first thing to consider is what type of individuals you are dealing with. What type of personality do they have in daily life? Are they the hardline, sales-type or are they deeply analytical, or are they more emotions based? If you ever find yourself searching for the right way to share information that may be less than optimal, I will give with you a very effective method that I have found works every time. Simply ask for permission to be honest.

Here are two scripts:

"Can I be honest with you about something?"

Or "Do I have your permission to be brutally honest with you?"

They will most often respond with "Yes." Raw honesty often exposes the full truth and facts in a deeply impactful way. The "rip the bandage off" method is great to use in just about every situation, because it gives your client a few seconds to brace for impact. In addition, the impact is usually much less than they expect. It is basic human behavior to think in worst-case scenarios, as it allows our brain to work from a position that ensures the best chance of survival. If ancient humans walked by a bush and the bush shook, their best chance for survival was to assume it was a saber-tooth tiger and not just the wind blowing through the leaves. Better to err on the side of caution and live than the exact opposite. Those instincts of survival are still at work in the human subconscious, even though the worst-case scenario in today's terms will not lead to a savage and bloody death in the jaws of a saber-tooth tiger, even though replacing that broken sewer line might cost a client $20,000.

Another advantage of this method of presenting the truth rather than sugar-coating or outright lying, is the respect factor. By asking them for their permission for you to be honest, you are being considerate of their emotions. If you break it down, they actually asked you for the truth by giving you their permission to share. I realize that this may seem elementary, but until you are in the sales trenches and are confronted with having to deliver bad news, you have no idea how hard it is. I have been involved in transactions where at some point, usually at the closing table, the buyers or sellers sitting on the opposite side of the table from me have finally received the blunt force truth from their agent, usually about some aspect of the transaction that the agent glossed over, and I will tell you it is not pretty. Upon learning the truth, no matter how minute it may be, other agent's clients usually get very upset and react in a way that can best be described as a prehistoric human being surprised by a saber-tooth tiger. This next common part of the story is both sad and true. Most times their agent—the one who withheld the information in the first place—will actually raise his or her voice, usually with a statement like, "I told you this," or "We discussed this; don't you remember?"

Pure and total hogwash. It is the agents' J-O-B to make sure that their clients have a crystal-clear understanding of every aspect of the transaction. Trust me when I tell you that you must prepare yourself to be honest and truthful with your clients, because delivering honesty is hard when you would rather spare your client the pain of bad news. Whether it is something about a price reduction, an inspection, trouble with loan approval, or presenting a lowball offer; when the time comes, you *owe* it to your clients to be prepared with the techniques and mindset to be honest in all dealings.

The only real flaw that exists with permission-based honesty is that you have to have some sort of rapport with whoever you are interacting with. If you have not established even a slight rapport and some basic trust, it can come off as rude.

For example, imagine yourself sitting in a restaurant where you have never eaten before. You have already finished your meal and you found it to be delicious, but you still have some room for dessert. You have been looking over the dessert menu for some time, when the waiter, who has been very attentive, prompt, and courteous, appears and asks, "Do we know what we want for dessert?"

At this point you still cannot seem to make up your mind. You very rarely order dessert, so you want something great and do not want to be disappointed. You have narrowed it down to two items: the cherry cheesecake and the chocolate mousse volcano explosion.

You ask the waiter, "Can I ask your opinion?"

The waiter says, "Absolutely!"

You ask, "Have you had the cherry cheesecake or the chocolate mousse volcano explosion before? Which one's better?"

The waiter responds, "Yes, and they are both good, but let me ask you, do you like bananas?"

You say, "Actually, yes, I love bananas."

Then the waiter asks, "Can I be honest with you?"

"Sure," you snappily reply.

The waiter then explains that the restaurant has been known for many years for its bananas Foster, and that it has actually won culinary awards around the globe for its bananas Foster. The one catch is that it is a bit of a secret, and it does not list it on the menu. You have to know to ask for it.

Without hesitation you say, "Yep, that is it, I will have the bananas Foster."

The waiter then says, "Just so you know, it does cost almost twice as much as the other desserts you were considering before. Is that okay?"

Again, without hesitation you say, "Oh, that is fine. I will have the bananas Foster."

"It'll be out shortly." The waiter speeds off to put in the order.

Before you realize it, the guy sitting at the table next to yours stands up to leave, and as he walks by your table, he leans over and says, "Can I be honest with you?" and continues without waiting for a response. "I wouldn't pay double for no dessert," he says and then lumbers out the front door.

How do you feel about your decision? I mean, both the waiter and the other patron are practically strangers to you. You have talked to the waiter only slightly more than with the other guy.

If I had to, I would guess that you probably still feel great about your dessert choice and that you cannot wait to annihilate it with your spoon. As for the unsolicited advice from a jackass who cannot mind their own business, it probably meant nothing, and you put no stock in what that moron said. Why? Because even the slightest bit of rapport builds enough trust for permission-based honesty.

Another top agent technique that is very effective in client communication usually makes most salespeople nervous and uncomfortable. It is a technique I learned in my first sales role decades ago, and it is completely nonverbal. The fact that it is nonverbal is what makes it so hard for most salespeople to use it, because we salespeople do like to talk. Some may argue that we old sales dogs are just trying to share information, but my research confirms that salespeople like to talk, mostly because we hate silence. We are human, and when there is a point of silence during a conversation involving humans, it is in our nature to become a bit jumpy and start talking, especially salespeople! I assure you that if you are a salesperson, especially a real estate salesperson, you need to learn the technique I'm about to tell you. Okay, here it goes. When you present your clients with good, solid, fact-based, truthful information, they will need some time to digest it. Also, when you present your client with information or a question that might require some time to think to arrive at a decision, you absolutely must use the following technique. To effectively use the technique, you will need to lower your top lip and press it firmly, but not too firmly, against your bottom lip. As I explained, don't press your top lip too firmly against your bottom lip, because you do not want to appear to be holding your breath, and you might forget to breathe and pass out. Do not do that. Relax, with lips pressed together (top agents call this pursing your lips) and use this script:

"..
........................"

Got it? As salespeople, I am sure doing that was difficult. You might take some time to reread the above paragraph again, just to be sure that you got it.

I am joking (mostly) and wanting to use some levity to illustrate the art of using silence, but with that said, it is only funny because it is so true. Most sales consultants have yet to master the use of silence to better serve their clients. Trust me, you will be serving them by shutting up and providing them with some silence to think, reflect, and contemplate the item or decision at hand. First of all, silence serves as the gateway for nonverbal communication. If you yip-yap on and on, neither your client nor you can read body language or feel the energy in the room, especially when trying to come to a decision. Remember that silence is good in that it leaves people with only their immediate thoughts. The thoughts that will either lead them to a decision or lead them to ask you questions or for your advice on the matter. As an example, when I find myself lost while driving, I need to turn off the radio and ask for some quiet in the car, just for a minute or two, while I get my bearings. As well, when I am learning something new, I find that I learn faster in a quiet environment. I know it is dangerous to project yourself onto the universe and claim that everyone acts as you do, but countless studies show that I am right. I have heard it said that in most situations, silence can do the heavy lifting, and in some cases, you have to just put the information out there and let the reality of what the information means appear to your client in their mind.

Another aspect to remaining silent does not require that you not speak, but that you do not say anything that you are not 100 percent certain of. There are three little words that act as kryptonite to even some of the best sales consultants in the business. What are they, you ask? Well, I will tell you, but first I must ensure that those salespeople who, in fact, do find these words to be their kryptonite are full prepared to see them, and if they can muster the power, to actually read them. Ready?

I

DON'T

KNOW

Everyone still with me? Are you all still doing well? Again, I am going to ask that you move up the page a few spaces and read those three words again, but this time, read them out loud. Ready?

Go!

Okay, are you all still good? Has anybody turned blue in the face? If so, please dial emergency services in your area or breathe into a small paper bag. We will respectfully wait for those of you who need the time.

The truth is that no reasonable person expects anybody to know everything. It is unrealistic and, quite frankly, impossible for a real estate agent, even a top real estate agent, to know everything there is to know about every possible real estate scenario, such as the bylaws of every homeowners association, the name of every school in a particular school district, or the square footage of a home you showed them a week ago Tuesday. If a client has that level of expectation, you need to reset that level and bring the client into the realm of reality. In extreme cases, you may better serve a client with that level of expectations by discontinuing the professional relationship. Clients do have a reasonable expectation that you will provide the information, or at least seek it out in a timely manner. We may live in the information age, but not every bit of information, particularly specialized information, is available online and immediately at our fingertips. It may take some research and plain old detective work to dig it up. Being able to say "I don't know, but I will find out and get back to you later today" presents the opportunity to show your client that you are a real person, you are honest, and even though you may not have every morsel of information committed to memory, you can deliver the answers and information the clients need. If you are asked the same question a second time and you do not have the answer at hand, it is totally on you. Either have notes with you in a file, on your phone, or wherever the information needs to be so you can get to it almost immediately. Not knowing the answer to a question asked a second time is incompetence on full display.

Tuning into WIIFM

WIIFM is not a radio station. I hope that as you read this in the future, radio stations will not have all disappeared and gone to an online format. Anyway, WIIFM is an acronym for the following: *What's In It For Me*. I am here to tell you, everybody wants to listen to that station (online or however). The basic tenant of every proposition is the simple and time-tested feature/benefit model.

For example, if you were in the market for some paint for your home, a feature/benefit might be:

FEATURE: This paint provides a long-lasting shine and finish that molecularly bonds to surfaces and will stand up to all nature can dish out.

BENEFIT: You will not have to spend the money or time to paint again for a long time.

It is the measuring stick that consumers use when deciding if the value of an item is equal to or greater than the cost. WIIFM is directly linked to a person's motive. You might be wondering so what? There is a reason why a person's objectives and motives matter. As a sales consultant and one who serves clients, it is paramount that you know your client's objectives and motives. You must discover their motivation and what they are trying to accomplish. The best way to do it is to ask. I am not trying to be cute here. You have to take control of the process early on and get your clients to open up about their motivation and objectives in a clear and specific way, covering the entire spectrum of what they need to accomplish. Top real estate agents know this fact and have in place a pre-listing or pre-buying consultation process. Most times it involves more than just one meeting. Top agents use online questionnaires that they request be completed prior to meeting. They typically provide their clients with an appropriate pre-listing or pre-buying information package as a thought starter. Top agents also gather information through phone screenings and a host of other information-gathering steps leading up to an in-person meeting. By positioning these steps and explaining that they will ultimately save time in the long run, top agents get the cooperation of their clients early on in the process. People are hard-wired to cooperate with each other for the common good, especially when people understand WIIFM. The reality is that both buying and selling a home is a very complex process that requires complete co-operation between client and agent, as well as the lender, title officer, and countless others along the way. It is critical that you set the tone of cooperation with your client from the beginning of the process. I choose to believe that most people are actually good and the world is full of good people, and I choose to work with good people, which is who I mostly encounter. The bottom line is that most people are helpful by nature to some degree and all are helpful when they understand what's in it for them.

A big question still remains. What does it take for most people to recognize and understand true value when it comes to things like being served?

It begins with having all the facts and information presented truthfully and clearly in a manner they can understand and digest. Another of the many keys to living a good life is making fact-based decisions. Without facts, we are reduced to impulse buyers, which only leads to some degree of dissatisfaction. People will also recognize true value when you set the dial to WIIFM. It is our job to ensure that all our clients have a full and complete understanding of the benefits of the options presented to them, and to effectively evaluate the options being offered, people must be given quiet time to reflect on what they have heard, seen, and experienced. If they cannot reach a decision, they need the quiet time to discover the questions they need answered and the additional bits of information they still need to make a fact-based, informed decision.

This entire chapter is dedicated to communication and how to effectively communicate with your clients and the people you have been entrusted with serving. If you boil it down to its essence, this chapter is really about coming from a place of contribution. This information gives a glimpse into understanding how to communicate with people in the language they understand, to help them accomplish their goals. Coming from contribution, or more simply, being a giver, swings the doors of communication wide open.

People Always Have Time for a Giver

When you conduct yourself as a giver, when you come from a place of contribution in all that you do, whether it is how you convey market information, show client appreciation, or send a simple "I was thinking of you" correspondence, you position yourself in a way that makes people want to reciprocate that behavior. To be clear, I am not speaking in terms of disingenuous motives, quid pro quo, or you scratch my back and I will scratch yours; actually, far from it. What I am saying is that because of your genuine acts of service, people will be less guarded, more open, and willing to engage with you. People are helpful and good natured. It is in our DNA. Humankind would have become extinct long ago if not for the inherent behavior of cooperation. This concept is the genesis of earning referrals and repeat business through serving others. One might even describe it as attracting or manifesting referrals and repeat business. I know I am walking up to the edge of a New-Age cliff; however you have got to hear what I am saying beyond the New Age, power of the mind hocus-pocus and focus clearly on the logic of conducting yourself as a contributor to all you come in contact with. It is important to understand this is precisely how we have successfully thrived as a species for thousands and thousands of years. We appreciate when others contribute to us personally, enhance our lives, and give to us, and in return, we humans love the chance to reciprocate that behavior and give back, to square up with those who help us. There it is. The secret of harmonious living is not keeping a detailed accounting of who owes you what, but rather seeking out those who you can help and paying it forward. Ultimately giving is a selfish act. I will say it again, so it sinks in: giving is an act of selfishness. A genuine, kind, positive, helpful, and prosperous act of selfishness, but an act of selfishness, nonetheless. We already know that people love tuning into WIIFM, but it not a bad thing. If done right, the formula for a good life consists of something like three parts contribution to one-part WIIFM. That formula would fill the world with abundance, prosperity, joy, and love.

Considering all that information, it quickly becomes abundantly clear why most people despise a taker, meaning those who take more than they contribute. We are wired within our DNA to cooperate with each other and believe that taking without giving is self-serving and will ultimately lead to the failure of all. Think about all the societal examples in movies and fables illustrating obnoxious greed. The stereotypical glutton, the Scrooge, the Monte Burns, as well as the prince of darkness, Satan, are all examples of those who take far more than they are willing to give back. This storyline has existed for millennia and has shown up throughout all of recorded history. Shaming and shunning the takers in society is really just an act of preservation to protect the collective.

Coming from contribution is not at all about exchanging forms of monetary value. In fact, the monetary items probably rank among the lowest that you can give. Not to say that giving anything of physical value is not appreciated. In the real estate agent's world those could be items such as a flyswatter, calendar, or a sports schedule, but they are really at the bottom of the pecking order. People like to know that they genuinely matter—more specifically, that they genuinely matter to you. One of the most powerful gifts you can give someone is to let them know that you are thinking of them. A note that says something like, "Hey, I saw this article and it made me think of you."

Or "I saw on Facebook that your kid won the championship. Way to go!"

Or "I saw on LinkedIn that you got a new job. Congratulations!"

Or "I'm so sorry for your loss of a loved one."

Most people would agree that when we read about events, accomplishments, and milestones in other people's lives, we often have an emotional reaction, so why not take it a step further and acknowledge it in a special or meaningful way? Send a quick handwritten note letting them know that you are aware of what is going on in their life and what is going on in the world that is important to them. A note like that one is equivalent to an analog "selfie" that they did not have to take.

Most acts of generosity of thought go much further than anything money can buy. Top agents are always on the lookout for developments that fall within the FORD profile with their people. FORD is an acronym that represents Family, Occupation, Recreation, and Dreams. Those are the top subjects on everybody's radar to one degree or another. Those categories often provoke thought because they are rooted in emotion. As sales consultants, we have a built-in need to present facts, figures, and logic, but logic makes people think, while emotion motivates people to get into action. Connecting on an emotional level with your people will therefore lead to an active relationship.

Emotion makes people act, and logic makes people think, but what makes people fire off to the moon like a rocket ship? Make no mistake; everybody has hot buttons, excitement chargers, nitro-adrenaline supersonic rocket launcher things in their lives. It usually turns out to be the most interesting thing about that person as well as the one thing that is the ultimate WIIFM item in that person's life. I want to take a minute to touch on something that all of us need in our lives and that is our one special thing. We are all focused on our loved ones, our spouses, our kids, our careers, our siblings, parents, company, church, charity, and on and on, but very few of us ever take time to solely focus on ourselves. I am not advocating a narcissistic, self-indulged focus, but investing some time in an area of our lives that is all about us. Even if it receives only an hour a month, it needs to be fed on a regular basis, to keep it alive. We all have it. Think back to when you were eight or ten or fifteen or twenty-five years old and ask yourself what was one of my passions, one thing that gave you a charge and still does. Not you the spouse, not you the parent or you the care giver, but *you*. We all have at least one thing that charges us up, gets us thinking, gets us talking and moving faster. What is it? The analogy of the airplane flight safety speech about putting on your oxygen mask before helping the others around you comes to mind as a fitting parallel to explain how we should live, at least a fraction of the time. As a side note, it is interesting that the airline industry actually has to *remind* us to be selfish enough to put on our oxygen mask, as an act of self-preservation, before helping others. The industry would not take the time to remind us if it was not necessary to, right? I said earlier that people are inherently good and hard-wired in their DNA to be good contributors to one another, and the fact that passengers would automatically help others before donning their own oxygen masks is just one glaring example of how true it actually is.

People have a deep, burning personal interest that can act like a shot of nitro-adrenaline for their soul. People do not typically share their deepest dreams and desires and passions with just everyone, but eventually you will learn, or at least observe, what it is. It will act as their ultimate emotional charge. It is probably the one area in life that most people will tolerate some healthy bragging from a humble hero. It is tolerated because people, especially our advocates in our life, want us to succeed, thrive, shine, and win. Everybody loves to be connected to a winner. If you do not believe me, then why do championship-winning teams always sell so much merchandise and people cover themselves in it? When was the last time you saw a crowd of people all decked out in runner-up gear? Exactly. Never. Since we are on the subject of healthy bragging and the humble hero, it is a complete disservice to our youth to participate in sports where everybody gets a trophy, everybody wins, and no one keeps score. Believe me when I tell you, everybody keeps score, even the little kids whose well-meaning parents and coaches do not. Life has winners and losers. Without losing, there is no need to improve and get better, faster, and stronger. There is no need to push yourself to be the best you are capable of. We collectively reward extreme performers. Look at how we hold top athletes, businesspeople, and philanthropists in such high regard. I am not advocating winning at all costs, but to better oneself, we must keep score, relish the victories as a humble hero, and be motivated by losses to learn and improve.

6

Never Work a Lead Again

Before we get far, it is important to distinguish what this chapter is all about and what it is not about. I am not wholly slamming the concept of buying and working to serve people who come to agents as leads from internet sources. Working online inquiries to serve the needs of buyers and sellers from internet lead sources is not bad on its face, especially in the case of real estate teams that have systems in place that can generate hundreds or even thousands of leads. However, keep in mind that these teams have specialized professionals and entire internet lead departments to handle the job. When operated at scale, there is definitely a case to be made that this area of the real estate industry is growing and is woefully underserved. What I take issue with is the single agent who has an entire database of clients that deserves the utmost and extreme attention and care. I have witnessed many agents trying to purchase a short cut to quick closes with a something-from-nothing strategy that accomplishes no more than wasting time and produces little or no return on investment. The favorite angle that the internet lead provider's sales staff love to use is the logic of by closing just one deal, the program pays for itself, but at what cost? Unless you have a specialized business strategy along with the budget and business volume to support internet lead-generation systems, the return on time does not pencil out as a winning strategy. Purchasing internet leads can be expensive in raw costs. If you are a team producing in the multiple tens of millions of dollars in production, internet leads are a way, albeit an expensive way, to expand your business. But working these leads effectively requires an immense amount of time as well as a specialized skillset that most individual agents do not possess. Think of it in terms of fishing. It is like comparing sports fishing to a commercial fishing operation. To make a profit catching a million pounds of fish takes specialized and expensive equipment, massive crews, elaborate processing plants, capital investments, and years of building the operation through trial and error, all while weathering the ups and downs of uncontrollable conditions at sea. A sport-fishing operation, that is to say, a person with a boat and three fishing poles, cannot hope to compete in the commercial marketplace. The case is nearly the same with fishing in a sea of internet leads. Contacting, nurturing, and serving the people who make up the internet leads that agents purchase is a complete business model in and of itself. The truth is that all agents, from the newly licensed in their first year to the seasoned professional doing a fair amount of business, have many people who go underserved, and the agents' focus should be squarely on serving those people first. It is a costly and, in some cases, a career-ending endeavor to jump into the internet-leads arena with both feet. Many agents who try to use internet leads as a quick fix actually try to use them as a way to avoid doing the work in the trenches. Believe me when I say that if it were possible to spend your way to prosperity by focusing on internet leads, it would have been done long ago, and 90 percent of us would have no market to serve.

In my experience, bulk internet leads are just one tier away from dialing through the white pages to prospect. Conversion rates of internet leads are advertised to be somewhere between 3 to 5 percent, meaning that for every one hundred leads that you buy, you can expect to find between three to five people to serve. Sounds good, but let's take a closer look at what is really behind those numbers. First of all, those numbers are what the industry publishes. I would say that 1 to 2 percent is more in line with reality, considering that most small teams and individual agents do not have a dedicated internet sales department. These leads come in at all hours of the day and most with incomplete information, so trying to reach these folks within the industry standard of five minutes or less is nearly impossible for a single agent to handle, considering that they probably are out showing houses, meeting clients, previewing homes, and handling all the day-to-day business dealings that agents perform. Logistically speaking, hitting that five-minute goal is quite a challenge. As well, many of the leads that come in are just people looking at houses as real estate voyeurs, so along with legitimate buyers, getting valid contact information or obtaining an email address that these voyeurs actually check and use is also an uphill battle. To be clear, internet leads can bring viable clients; however, the time and specialized talent it takes to convert them into clients is a losing battle when done on a small scale.

A better approach, and one that top real estate agents take, is to actually prospect for new people to serve. Actively prospecting for new people to serve is a much more solid foundation on which to build your real estate sales business. The National Association of Realtors® statistics show that the average American sells and buys a home roughly every seven years, so many of the people you come in to contact with are at some point on the seven-year spectrum, which is perfect timing to build a pipeline of clients to nurture and serve. It is much easier to have a dialog with someone you met at an open house or by door knocking than it is to try to spark a dialog with a person who registers as a lead. The conversation becomes especially challenging for an agent who is the third to have called within the last half hour because the person made the mistake of using his real cell phone number when he registered on 3 different real estate listing platforms. Simply put, working internet leads as a single agent is nothing more than chasing transactions, and chasing transactions is no way to build a business. Properly corresponding with internet leads in a timely and meaningful way is a grind, and it is thankless to boot. Traditional prospecting methods help agents lay solid groundwork to build a relationship based on loyalty. Even if agents do their best to come from contribution when working bulk internet leads, they still might show up as a taker.

I am positive that most agents are eager to serve; however it is difficult to overcome the stigma that an agent is calling an internet lead only to cash in on a sale. There is just no rapport built into the mix when it comes to following up with the people agents contact from internet lead sources, and those people tend to keep their defenses up, which is probably the reason for the low conversion rates and the specialized training needed to convert those leads.

If you are thinking that you do not have to make phone calls to stay in touch with your people, you are mistaken. I am not claiming that to be the case either. You will still have to engage in conversations with strangers at open houses, door knocking, community events, and with referrals. Conversion is a numbers game when prospecting for new people to serve. Your success in real estate sales is directly tied to the number of people who think about you when they think about real estate. That adage is as true today as was when I first read it in the book, *The Millionaire Real Estate Agent*. The concept of a numbers game is simple but by no means easy. The more people you initially meet, establish a rapport with, stay in contact with, and build a relationship with, the more success you'll have in the real estate business. Let's revisit the fishing analogy from earlier in this chapter.

Think of the real estate business like fishing in a pond. If a fisherman intends to catch the same amount of fish year after year, the pond must be consistently restocked with more fish, or the pond will become fished out and all the fish will eventually be caught. The case is the same with your database. Attrition, such as people moving away from your local market, clients obtaining a real estate license, clients' family member obtaining their real estate license, or endless other scenarios all takes a toll on the number of people in your database. Top agents are always prospecting for new people to serve. This is where the basic premise of business holds true: "If you aren't growing, you're dying."

You can ask your mother for client referrals only so many times before even she stops taking your calls.

Another great benefit of consistently prospecting for new people to serve is that prospecting gives agents a golden opportunity to be genuine. As discussed earlier, first impressions are hard to change. Top agents know that prospecting for clients is playing the long-term game. It demonstrates to people that the agent is service-based and has shown up in their life with the mission to serve. Top agents understand that this is an opportunity to let their unique style shine through. The majority of people you come into contact with will appreciate the truth of who you really are. People value genuine interaction. Sometimes a connection is made just because a person is sincere and genuine. Never underestimate most people's ability to spot the fake and disingenuous motives of the transactional-minded agent. Today's social-media environment is full of spur-of-the-moment photos, selfies, and all around "look at me" content that the average person probably sees a dozen or more examples of each and every day. In the day and age of staged lives and endless photo filters, genuine interactions are treasured.

Just as much as being "genuinely you" is appreciated, never lose sight of the fact that your content and interactions cannot be all about you. Always remain respectful, if you want to be respectable. Rule number one is always be nice. You never know what people may be going through the moment you show up in their life. One of my go-to prospecting strategies when I was newly licensed was door knocking. My script was very simple. I said, "Hello, I'm holding an open house at one twenty-three Main Street tomorrow from one to three. I'd like to let you know there may be some extra traffic in the neighborhood during those times, so if you have kids or pets, please be aware of the added traffic, because I market my open houses extensively. By the way, if you'd like to come and check it out, you're more than welcome to, and if you know anyone that wants to live in this great neighborhood, maybe you could "pick" your new neighbor by inviting your friends along."

One particular day I was making my rounds and door knocking the twenty-five homes surrounding my upcoming open house when I knocked on one particular door that completely changed my perspective forever. I knocked, he answered, and I got, "Hello, I'm holding an open house—" out of my mouth before he responded, "Get the f#*k off my porch," and then the front door slammed.

I was shocked. Yes, some people have been short with me or given a stern response of, "not interested," but I had never been treated so rudely for simply letting a neighbor know there was going to be an open house a few doors down. For a person to have such an explosive, rage-filled response to a small interruption in his day caught me off guard. My initial thought was to knock on the door again and give that guy a piece of my mind. In the few seconds that followed, I calmed down and decided to move on to the next door. As I turned to leave his front porch, however, I spotted what I had somehow missed when I walked up to the door a half minute earlier. Hanging in the window was a red-and-white pennant with a blue-and-white center and one gold star. The wars in Iraq and Afghanistan were raging, and I had just come into contact with a gold-star family member. I wondered, "How long has that gold star been in their window?" Perhaps it was hung a minute or two before I showed up. I will never know.

The lesson in that story is that we should never react to situations that we encounter when prospecting and always respond professionally, because we never know what other people may be dealing with the moment we show up in their lives.

Another hard-and-fast rule I abide by is never to use foul language with someone I intend to serve. Never. Sometimes it is tempting to do so, especially if people are cussing up a storm in a way that would make a sailor blush. I was told early on in my sales career that you will never get in trouble for what you do not say. In the instance of foul language, this adage applies precisely. The temptation to use the mirror-and-match communication technique to connect does not apply here. When using foul language in a business setting, one presents as unprofessional and unpolished. Avoid using foul language.

Through the course of effective prospecting there is a line that exists. As a matter of fact, a very fine line. This line should never be crossed. I am talking about the fine line between serving the public by offering up your expertise at the highest level and with the utmost skill and care and being a leg-humper.

Yes, you read that correctly, it says do not be a leg-humper. I am making reference to those who stoop so low as to beg, plead, and otherwise act out of desperation. Those agents, after making a solid initial contact, verbally pester, prod, poke, and harass people to death.

There are plenty of systems and formulas out there outlining how to effectively follow up with people you just met and immediately begin to earn their trust and cement a solid professional relationship. I have researched, used, and even developed a few of these systems, and not one of them prescribes contacting people multiple times in the first day or two after meeting them. Can you say psycho? I am reminded of the 1996 movie *Swingers*, where the main character, Mike, played by Jon Favreau, leaves five answering machine messages in a three-minute timeframe for a girl he met earlier that evening while he was at a club. As he was leaving the last message, explaining why he left the first four, the girl picks up the phone and says, "Never call me again" and hangs up on him.

It was a funny and uncomfortable scene, and it illustrates exactly what agents should not do when contacting a client they just met. To be clear there is the occasion where a new contact can turn into a highly motivated and immediate business relationship, which is not what I am talking about. I am referring to the casual exchange where a person says something like, "Hey, great meeting you. When our daughter graduates from high school in three years, we're gonna make a move. Please stay in touch."

Do not spoil the opportunity to forge a strong bond by being a leg-humper that whorishly thrusts himself upon every unwitting person who engages ever so slightly. In this same arena of thought, I offer the simple two-no rule when speaking with a prospect, particularly over the phone. The rule is simple to follow. An example of the two-no rule would go something like this: "Is there anybody you know whom I could help with real estate right now?"

No.

"How about you? Is there anything you need from me?"

No.

"Fantastic. We'll talk soon. Take care. Bye." Click.

Over the years I have seen a few call scripts that deviate from this formula and have listened in on a few painfully relentless calls that hound and hound people for referrals. Keep it simple and stick to the two-no rule. You will thank me later.

On the other side of the spectrum of going out of your way to serve those you prospect is giving too much too freely. I call it being a pop-tart or a cheap date who says yes to anything and everything. In this business, and for that matter throughout your life, you teach other people how you want to be treated by the boundaries you set. Many times an agent's actions and words are way out of alignment in this area. It seems that the same agents who make statements to their clients like, "I'm always available to my clients" Or "You can call me whenever; I'm here for you" end up being the exact same agents who complain when their clients call or text them at all hours expecting an immediate response.

It is critical that you establish boundaries early and up front about the hours you are available and what a client should expect when it comes to how and when you will respond to their calls, texts, and emails. For those of you who are first starting out, resist the temptation to pop up at any given request from a client. By setting boundaries, you establish a business relationship that is respectful of your time and schedule. With that said, I get it. I was a new agent once too. Just know that every time you drop everything on a moment's notice and meet a stranger to show any random property, you are teaching the client how to treat you. This lesson usually has to be learned the hard way, but bear in mind that every interaction with a prospect or client will set a precedent for future interactions. Avoid creating a monster of unmanageable expectations that will quickly grow out of control as your business activity grows.

You should be protective of giving your time, trust, and commitment, because there are many time wasters in the world today. Remember that those we aim to serve will usually guard themselves as well. Many people you are prospecting will work to protect themselves from a perceived waster of their time, trust, or commitment. It has nothing to do with you, so do not take it personally. You may put together an item of value, such as a quarterly neighborhood sales report, a small gift, or an event, and you will find some people are not receptive to your offerings or even outright refuse to accept them. They might say "I'm not interested" or "No, thank you."

Again, do not take it personally; they are just protecting themselves from committing to you or they do not want to end up in a perceived quid pro quo scenario where they feel they owe you something. Assure them that you share this information with a lot of your contacts, and they find it useful or that there is no obligation or any of the dozens of things you can say to have them drop their barriers and engage. However, do not forget the two-no rule and remain respectful and respectable.

One of the other items that people have become very protective of is their contact information. If people are not ready to share their contact information, that is okay. If you have their name, try engaging them through social media. If you have their address because you met them door knocking in their neighborhood, try engaging them with a simple letter or postcard. Always stop short of being a creeper. There are many services out there where you can find loads of personal information, cell phone numbers, email addresses, birthdays, and so on. Do not freak out people you barely know by sending them an anniversary card or calling to wish them a happy birthday. There is a line that can easily be crossed, so make sure you have their minimum permission to engage with them beyond your initial interaction.

Prospecting for new people daily and in a systematic way is a real estate business essential, and mathematically speaking, the odds will be in your favor. Over the years I have unscientifically discovered a few of the percentages and numbers you can count on to be true when engaging with people while prospecting, regardless of which prospecting activity you are engaged in. About three people out of one hundred will give a cold response when you try to engage with them. And about two out of one thousand people will be "hass-oles" and give you a hassle for even thinking that you are worthy to speak with them. What top agents know is that about 70 percent of the people will engage cordially. The other nearly 30 percent, at the moment you make contact, are not ready, willing, or able to engage and will not respond cordially. Bottom line, in my experience most people are nice and will respond in kind, even if there is no chance that you will ever serve as their agent.

I have done extensive field research in the business of real estate sales, and I will now share this invaluable information with you in these next few paragraphs. This research was extremely costly, and I would personally like for you to benefit from the exhaustive and extensive research that I have paid for in time and, most notably, treasure. Ready?

You cannot spend your way to prosperity.

Early in my career I signed many contracts and marketing agreements and signed up for countless programs, customer resource management databases, and websites. As well, I have paid anywhere from $20 each to well over $100 each for leads. I will repeat this statement with 100 percent certainty: *You cannot spend your way to prosperity.*

First of all, think about it logically. If it were as simple as buying the right leads or finding the right program to make it rain clients and home sales, real estate agents would have gone extinct fifty years ago. If it were possible, some brokerage or a handful of top producers would have cornered the market with the mythical, magical sales-generating machine, and we would all be working for them now. Logically speaking, if it were possible, it would have been conceived, developed, implemented, signed, sealed, and delivered long, long ago. Quite frankly it is a big part of why I took the time to write a book about how Zillow.com, Realtor.com, Trulia.com, Homes.com, or any other entity cannot spend their way to prosperity in the real estate business. Sure, agents should make sensible investments in their business. But the idea that a person could obtain a real estate sales license, subscribe to a program from a lead service provider, and voilà, overnight go from having zero clients to being a mega producer is just plain illogical. There is a robust real estate lead generating industry out there that makes billions of dollars off the false promise to agents that they can spend the commission from closing "just one more deal a year" to reap dozens and dozens more transactions a year. Only one side of that equation is getting paid, and it is not the side of the agents writing checks and waiting for clients and closings to appear magically.

Hands down, the number-one most cost-effective way to prospect for new clients in the real estate business is the open house. Holding open houses offers endless opportunities for those willing to put in the work. When I say open house, I am referring to an event. There is a huge difference between banging a couple of signs in the ground and unlocking the front door verses turning an open house into an extravaganza. Open houses offer the opportunity of leverage. The sky (and an agent's creativity) is the limit. Agents use open houses as an opportunity to door knock; put out loads of branded signage; and co-op with lenders, stagers, home warranty companies, and title reps to offer refreshments, have raffles, offer prizes, and turn the volume up to eleven. As well, open houses are hyper-geographical, meaning that if agents want to establish their business in a given area, they should focus all their open-house efforts in that area. No listings? No problem! Approach top producers with listings in the area and offer to hold their listings open. In return, perhaps offer them a nice report that outlines the day's activities and results that they can easily brand with their own information and provide to their clients. Offer to make them look like the hero to their clients while you are able to establish a name for yourself in the area. Holding an open house is the best venue to showcase your talents, skills, knowledge, and ability to market homes at a high level. It is an opportunity to show an entire neighborhood of prospects why they should hire you to market, list, and sell their home. Holding high-level open houses is the fastest way to build your business, hands down. In chapter nine I will go into greater detail about how to conduct effective open houses.

The underlying theme when prospecting is always to be looking for an approach that comes from a point of contribution. As a species, human beings are hard-wired to cooperate with one another. We have developed societal systems over millennia that are rooted in cooperation. Our economic systems, our educational systems, our paring/coupling/marital systems, communities, organizations, unions, and associations are all based on cooperation. As humans cooperating is what we do best. As well as being hard-wired to cooperate to contribute to the common good, coming from a point of contribution reveals your base motivations. When your base motivation is to serve, it will shine through without question. Because we are hard-wired to cooperate for the common good and come from contribution, it feels good to contribute. Simply put, a prospecting and business philosophy rooted in the idea of coming from a point of contribution fulfills our mission as a human. Our mission is to help fellow humans succeed and prosper.

One thing to keep in mind when trying to do basic prospecting by purchasing leads is that there is a low probability of a long-term relationship when you "just pay for it." There are many analogies I could employ here, but I am sure that you can think of them without my help or colorful word pictures. Buying leads commoditizes your value proposition. Paid leads have a short shelf-life and require a specialized skillset to convert them consistently. Ultimately it is just a difficult way to start a relationship that must be rooted in loyalty and trust.

7

Saying Thank You

The mindset of a giver is, in a word, gratitude. The heart of a giver is full, even bursting with joy-filled thankfulness for all things: for the sun that warms us, the food that nourishes us, and the others who have come before us and passed on their knowledge. Perhaps they are even thankful for their kids, pets, spouse, partner, parents, grandparents, and friends; for wealth, their country of origin, their adopted country, their opportunities, and on and on. These are all wonderful things to be grateful for. People have known for centuries that just a few minutes of a focused, daily expression of gratitude improves a person's overall quality of life; however, to sum up the mindset of a giver is to say that a giver is grateful for the opportunity to serve others. A giver knows that opportunities to serve show up every day and are easy to spot with little or no effort. Throughout my years in the real estate business I have seen the most masterful plans and best of intentions to serve the public with genuine gratitude in mind. Many programs and contributions have been proposed, thought up, formulated, and designed, from donating a portion of an agent's commission to a specific charity to supporting the local Parent-Teacher Association to conducting food drives to executing one gratis transaction a year for a seller in need. I believe that the intention is almost always, or at least 99 percent of the time, heartfelt and genuine. I also believe that to the best of my recollection and mental accounting, about the same number, 99 percent, are never implemented, or at best implemented for a blink of an eye and never followed through on. As we have discussed, most agents approach this business from a transactional mindset, which over time can become hollow and cold. In the instances of agents that actually did follow through on their plans, their efforts were always impactful. Show, rather than tell, is probably the best approach when it comes to giving of time and effort to community. Keller Williams Realty participates in an event called Red Day every May 15, and brokerages all over the country as well as brokerages internationally participate in a day dedicated to serving their communities. This annual event is excellent, and when well-executed at the brokerage level can make a huge impact on other peoples' lives, but that type of giving of one's time, talent, and treasures are by nature infrequent and rare, for nothing else than the lack of our most precious commodity: time. The mindset of a giver is focused on giving back to those around them through tiny, subtle, meaningful actions that serve those around them. Actions speak volumes, and words are limited to conveying thoughts, promises, and ideas. In this chapter we are going to take a look at the endless ways your real estate practice provides you with the opportunity to serve the public, your people, clients, and all others with a gratitude-based, heartfelt approach. That approach will serve those all around you at a high level and also do great things for you as a human being.

The Power of a Handwritten Note

The handwritten note is becoming quite a lost artform as a way to communicate. Whether it is to say thank you or to congratulate someone for a recent accomplishment or to merely say "I was thinking of you," a handwritten note is unrivaled at making a big, and sometimes seismic, impact on someone and brightening their day, week, or even perhaps their whole year. I have special little cards and envelopes that I use, but when I started doing this little gem of a communication style, I started by using a single piece of printer paper stuffed in a legal envelope. I believe that my fancy little notecards embossed with my name that I use today have made zero difference in how my handwritten messages are received. Personally I prefer the small notecards over the printer paper, because the cards are easier for me to handle and I like the limited space they give for my message. It is said that brevity is the soul of wit. When it comes to writing effective notes to others, brevity is probably the most important rule. The action of handwriting two to five sentences to say thank you or congratulations or condolences or just thinking of you goes far in communicating that you are genuine and heartfelt in how you serve others. I have shared this little gem with thousands of other business people throughout the decades, and not one person that I can recall thought that it was a bad idea. In fact, almost everybody thinks it is an exciting way to come from contribution. But guess what. Hardly anybody does it. I hold out hope that one day I will get at least one thank-you note thanking me for the handwritten-note idea. Not because I am on some sort of ego trip or something, but because it is easily the first note that anyone could write and would be a wonderful first step in taking up the habit of note writing. I have never specifically asked any of my audience members to send me a note, but if you are paying attention, drop me a quick note to my business address:

Scott Futa
Keller Williams Realty Success
2650 W. Belleview Ave. #300
Littleton, CO 80123

I promise I will read it and, with much gratitude, write you back, provided you attach a return address. A quick and specific word of advice when it comes to writing an effective note: do not include any-thing that is business related, such as your logo or your business card or anything else that would imply that you are asking for something in return. If you need to address such things or matters specific to busi-ness, email would be the appropriate way to go. A handwritten note can best be described as a "literary hug," so do not ruin it by turning it into a sales pitch. Even if you do not mean it that way, it is easy to muddy the intent of the message by injecting business. Turning the practice of sending short, simple, handwritten notes into a habit of sending one to five notes each day has the power to change your life. More than that, each note you send will bring joy into your life ten-fold more than those who are on the receiving end, and those on the receiving end will be blown away with gratitude to have received it. Send out some simple notes and see what happens. I dare you!

The Purpose of a Gift

When I think of the word *gift*, the first things that come to mind are birthdays and holidays. I will bet that I am not alone in that. Ever since most of us can remember, from our childhood until today, receiving gifts happens on our birthday or the holidays. The tradition in Western culture has been of gift-giving on these occasions, perhaps the most exciting events involve gift-giving. But have you ever stopped to think about what a gift represents? What does the giving of a gift actually communicate? To be honest, I never gave much thought to what the giving of a gift actually communicated to the receiver. In the course of completing countless real estate sales transactions, I have given countless closing gifts. Until recently I never stopped to give thought to what I was actually trying to say to my clients by giving them a gift, I guess because in Western culture giving gifts has become sec-ond nature, perhaps even mundane and routine. When my sons were younger and invited to a birthday party, we bought some sort of gift for the unknown chap, usually with our son's guidance. Sometimes we give someone a gift out of a sense of obligation, like when your kind-of-familiar neighbor brings over a fruit cake during the holidays (obviously regifted by the telltale bits of tape on the bottom of the tin), you feel an obligation to reciprocate. I have even resorted to buying a few generic emergency gifts for just such an occasion. This year the emergency gifts were a few small boxes of peppermint chocolates that I wrapped up. Everybody loves a coffee shop gift card stuck in a coffee cup, if nothing else, to regift. In taking the time to think about gifts and what they actually communicate, I have boiled it down to two main reasons that most people give gifts. They do it either to communicate that they value someone or that they want to congratulate them. To take it further, who do we give gifts to in the course of doing the business of real estate sales? That too I boiled down to two main types: closing gifts for buyers and sellers and thank-you gifts for those who refer business. Strangely enough, both those types of gifts are a token of congratulations as well as an expression of valuing a relationship. The final aspect of the act of gift giving we will look at is a gift given to memorialize an occasion. To bring all of this information back to the business of real estate and gratitude and all of that stuff, the two most common types of gifts in the real estate business are closing gifts and referral gifts.

As far as closing gifts go, there are many philosophies out there as to what is appropriate and what is not. There are also limits to how much the Internal Revenue Service allows you to deduct for a gift. As for my approach, I tend to listen to clients and get them something they may bring up during the course of the transaction. Some examples are electronic keypads, a dog door installation, or some prepaid handyman services. If you are trying to avoid a standard and clichéd closing gift, turn toward your client's kids or pets. Doing something nice for a client's schnauzer or little Billy or Suzie can mean much more than any gift you might give to your client directly. I am on the practical side and avoid expensive Champagne, perishable flowers, or expensive candy. Never forget some essential items that everyone can use while in the process of moving. Toilet paper, a flashlight, lightbulbs, road snacks, paper towels and plates, disinfectant or spray cleaner, along with some other essentials can be assembled in a clothes basket and made into a thoughtful, creative, and relatively inexpensive closing gift. Some agents give no closing gift other than the best service and experience, and that is okay too, although the opportunity to show a little gratitude is staring you right in the face, but it is still okay. It seems that a closing gift can be about as unique and diverse as the individual agent. The second gift to consider, and in my experience the more important one, is the referral gift. In the case of the referral gift, it must reward the behavior of generously giving you referrals. First off, it is critical that you reward the action of the referral and not wait until the transaction has closed. Think about what a big mistake it is to wait until closing to thank someone for the referral. You are rewarding them only if you receive compensation, which is not the goal of having people refer business. First off, top real estate agents know that the behavior to reward is the action of sending an opportunity to do business and serve a client. And secondly, by the time you sit at the closing table, side-by-side with referred clients, months could have passed since the clients were referred to you, in which time I guarantee you the person who referred the clients to you has probably forgotten that they sent you the referral. If you do not show those who refer business to you how big a deal and how grateful you are for their referral, I can all but promise your referral business will be nonexistent. If you would like to wait until closing to send them something real nice, by all means you can do that, but you must acknowledge the actual referral with fanfare and grandiosity. Hear me when I tell you this: *The Immediate Reward for the Referral Is All That Matters*. Sure, it could be nice to send a little something to referrers after you close a person they sent to you, but that is not actually rewarding the behavior of sending you referrals. I am positive that if people are taking the time to send you referrals, they probably like you and trust you, so they are not looking for some expensive, elaborate gift. However, it is critical that you send them a gift that conveys the sentiment of how much you value them and how much you appreciate that they would even think of you. After all, they are thinking of you and your business by taking the time to refer people to you.

A referral gift should be personal, within reason. With that said, it is easy to overthink the action of gift giving to reward a referral. At the very least, the gift should show that you know something about the recipient. I know of a few cases where agents have sent wine to recovering alcoholics and a pound of exotic coffee to a family that does not drink caffeine. Gifts like that will most certainly have the opposite effect of telling them that you value their relationship. In fact, it says "I hardly know you, but I send this to everyone, so if you do not like it, no big deal, just regift it next Christmas to your neighbor." At all costs avoid sending the message that the referral was no big deal, because if you do, believe me, they will stop sending referrals your way.

Another best practice when it comes to receiving referrals is making a follow-up phone call to say thank you again. It cannot be stressed enough how important referrals are to the health of your business. They are the essential lifeblood of the real estate business, and it cannot be overstated that you must make your referral partners know that their referrals are a big deal. I say double the love. Send them a gift immediately and also follow up to thank them voice-to-voice. This question comes up a lot actually: "What if they called you to give you the referral?" Okay, thank them on the first call, send them a gift immediately, and then call shortly after the referral, maybe a week, to give a simple update on how things are going and thank them again.

A word of caution: it is critical that you never discuss the private business between you and the referred client. It is a breach of your duties to the client, and it is poor form. The reason it is so important to follow up with a phone call after about a week is that the people may have another referral for you. If they did it once, with your encouragement, they will most likely do it again.

In making this call, and in all gift-giving, it is so important that you avoid even insinuating a quid-pro-quo scenario, the old, "I'll scratch your back if you scratch mine" dynamic. Even if it is a business-to-business referral from your inspector or carpet guy or your go-to painter, never insinuate quid pro quo. It is tacky and it feels disingenuous, even if you do not mean it that way. I promise, these people know what you do, so there is no need to remind them that "my business is built on referrals and who do you know that I can help?"

Reward their behavior and make a big deal out of the referral, prospect them for more business another day, and definitely not while you are in the process of thanking them.

Here's another little tidbit for you about conveying gratitude and showing that you value referral and client relationships. Always avoid the word *thanks*. Drop the *s* and add *you*. *Thank you*. There are reasons that you need to be careful with just saying or writing *thanks* when communicating gratitude. First reason, it sounds kind of fake and not at all heartfelt. Second, it gives the impression you are merely acting out of obligation. It sounds that way. Third and most important, it leaves out the most important person in the equation: them! Let's get real here for a second. Picture a thirteen-year-old who you might know, or might have known, who is super obnoxious in a thirteen-year-old kind of way, for whom you might have done something nice for, and the kid just turns to you momentarily and, in a nasally voice, screeches out "Thaaanks." Yeah, I think you get the drift. When communicating gratitude always write out the words *thank you*.

Timing should not be overlooked when sending a gift or a thank you note because it is no understatement to say that thank-you notes do not age well. Obviously a delayed or late thank-you gift can give the impression that the whole thing was not important to you at all. It is clear that the things we pay attention to are the things that matter most to us, and the things we forget are usually low priority. If you want to last in the real estate business, you'd better make every aspect of your referral business a top priority. A late or delayed referral gift or thank-you card makes it clear that you are unorganized and forgetful of those who kindly help you in building your business. Do not ever appear to be someone who just takes, and a delayed thank-you card or referral gift communicates just that.

I understand that we all make mistakes. I will admit that I have made my fair share of boneheaded mess ups. So, if you overlook sending a thank-you gift to someone in a timely manner, by all means call and apologize. Thank them for the referral and for thinking of you and then drop them something to show your gratitude. In the ultra-rare case when this happens, do not freak out. We are, after all, human, and we will all make mistakes. And remember, mistakes are only 10 percent about the actual mistake and 90 percent about how you rectify the mistake. May I suggest a display of humility, honesty, and class, as those three attributes will get you far in the real estate business when you mess up.

As your business grows, so will your referral business. Be mindful that you should start early with a simple system to systematically send gifts and thank-you cards. It is very important to be consistent in giving gifts and rewards. Some people are super competitive, and you might be shocked at what lengths some people will go to make sending referrals a game and send as many referrals to you as they can. Some people actually will keep score in their heads as to how many referrals they have sent you or how many gifts they can get by sending you referrals. Another thing to consider is that if you follow your system perfectly a few times and then slack a bit, the person sending the referrals will definitely notice. By being inconsistent, you create the potential to appear unorganized, ungrateful, or both. Haphazardly giving gifts, inconsistently sending thank-you cards, and following up intermittently will make the rewards and gratitude seem like an afterthought. Get a system, write it down, implement it, and remain consistent.

Something special to consider for someone who sends you multiple referrals is a scaled reward system. A scaled reward system is simply a system in which the rewards get more and more extravagant with each referral. This type of system works really well with the super-competitive people who send you referrals, because they appreciate the opportunity to compete. For those who send you referrals that result in many transactions, it is a great way to say thank you in a big way. Be sure that you understand and comply with The Real Estate Settlement Procurement Act of 1974 (RESPA).

This chapter has been loaded with time-tested approaches to the giving gifts, but from time to time, your clients will give you a gift. I know, right? Whaaat? I have been shocked and surprised by clients I have provided such a great experience that they not only agree to pay me a commission but also want to give me a gift. As a focused giver, it is easy to feel a bit shy to receive, or more directly to take from those that we serve, but in these situations, you must be a gracious receiver. Clients sometimes are so overwhelmed with happiness and gratitude—in fact bursting with it—that they will stop at nothing to pass out thank-you gifts to everyone. They give a gift to their lender, their title representative, their closer, and whoever else is at the closing. Whenever this happens, it can feel unnatural for those you serve and protect to reward you. After all, it is your job to take care of your clients that way. Whatever you do, do not refuse their gift in an attempt to be nice, because doing so will come off as a rejection of them and will ultimately deny them their expression of gratitude. By graciously accepting their gift, you are giving them the ultimate form of gratitude. Be a gracious receiver too.

Referrals; It's What's for Business

Like the deep voice says in the commercial, "Beef; it's what's for dinner," I say, "Referrals are what's for business." Many years ago I was following up with a past client who had just referred a neighbor to me. Through the course of the conversation, we discussed how life was going and exchanged updates on our kids and our families. At some point during our conversation I made the comment, "Hey, Cody, I want to thank you again for sending that referral our way."

Before I could say another word, he stopped me and said, "Scott, I did not send you a referral; you earned it. Every person I send your way is because you work hard to keep earning my business, so I know when I send someone your way, you are going to take care of them. I don't give you anything; you earn it."

8

You Must Earn Business; You Do Not Just 'Get' It

How is *earning* a result of *giving*? What a simple question, or it appears to be. Think about it a bit deeper and really put some thought into the answer. *How is earning a result of giving*? On the surface the question seems simple. A person might answer with this example, "Let's assume some dude walks into a store wanting a snack. He decides he wants a cookie. He selects the cookie he wants, carries it to the clerk, pays the clerk for the cookie, walks out of the store, and eats the cookie. By *giving* the clerk the payment for the cookie, the dude *earned* the right to eat it."

In a very basic sense, that answer might be a correct, but it sounds more like the description of a transaction. It is clear that the act of *transacting* is simply an exchange of value. But if you think about it on a deeper level, *earning* is an exchange of value as well, but in a different form. Let's go back to the earlier answer about the cookie. I do not know about you, but the cookie example has me picturing some dude walking into a random convenience store, likely a chain franchise, impulsively wanting snack. He sees a cookie on the counter for some price, probably under a buck, buys it, eats it, and without much thought or fanfare goes about his day. Now let's take a minute and think about a different buying experience involving a cookie. And folks, this one happened to me. Yes, I am admitting it now, for all of the world to read, to pass judgment and condemn me for the stupidity, my stupidity that I am about to reveal to the world. I once paid $18 for a single cookie. Yes, you read that correctly, I once paid $18 for a single cookie. Not to belabor the point, however, if I include the taxes and tip, the purchase of a single cookie came out to roughly just over $20. Now before anyone gets all geographic and "economies of scale" on me, this was in Denver, Colorado. The transaction was not made on the island of Manhattan or in the City by the Bay, where everything seems to be much more expensive. It was Denver. It went down like this: After a very nice dinner with my lovely wife, the valet brought our car around. We got in the car, and as I slowly drove out of the parking lot about 9:45 p.m., visions of my bed began floating in my head. To be clear, I had just finished a very large steak dinner and was not hungry at all. In fact I was stuffed, but little did I know I was mere moments away from paying almost twenty bucks for a cookie. As my wife snapped her seatbelt, she blurted out, "Oh, I heard about this great dessert spot just down the street. Let's go." Being the good husband that I am (actually if you ask me, my wife won the husband lotto), I replied, "Sure. Which way?"

She excitedly said, "Left!"

The important detail here is that to go home I had to turn right, so now I was driving out of my way to get dessert that I was too full to eat anyway, but I was taking one for the team. After all, she is always looking out for me, taking care of me (read: putting up with me), so the least I could do was get her some dessert, right?

About ten minutes later, in the opposite direction of home (where my bed is located), we finally pulled up to the place, but there was not any parking out front, so I drove past the place and pulled down the very next side street, turned, and then drove down half a block to park. We walked up the block, around the corner, and halfway down that block to the dessert bar. We walked in, and I was blown away. The place had to be a five-star dessert restaurant. The lighting, décor, and overall ambiance was perfect. We were seated and given menus. After a quick scan of the menu, I shrugged my shoulders and mouthed the words, "I could eat."

It was then that something caught my eye. That something was the word *snickerdoodle*. You see, my mom was a working mom, a nurse. She worked hard, so she did not spend much time in the kitchen baking, but when she did, her go-to cookie recipe was for snicker-doodles. Just as I was contemplating the cinnamon cookie goodness that a snickerdoodle has to offer, the waiter appeared at our table and asked if we were ready to order. My wife replied, "Scott, you go first. I'll be ready in a sec."

I asked, "What can you tell me about the snickerdoodle?"
"Well, the cookies are fresh-baked because we do a batch about ev-ery half hour…" At this point the waiter's voice became a droning rhythm (imagine Charlie Brown's teacher's voice) and the smell, that sweet cinnamon smell, which I had not noticed until then, hit me. The waiter finished with something about vanilla bean ice cream or something, and I replied, "Yeah, I'll have that."

He then turned to Sarah and took her order. I do not remember what she ordered. He retrieved our menus and took off.

As we sat in our booth, we sipped our coffees and chatted. I was eagerly awaiting the dessert. Shortly thereafter, the waiter appeared again with two full-size plates. One held whatever my wife had ordered, and the other one was for me. The plate seemed to gleam in the dim light as the other patrons murmured conversations around me and the piano jazz music pumped from the speakers hidden somewhere in the ceiling. The waiter set the plate in front of me, slightly tilting it as he let it down on the table, causing a bit of the pile of vanilla bean ice cream, slightly melted by the warmth of the freshly baked manhole-cover-sized snickerdoodle cookie, to pool near the lip of the plate. I remember grabbing my fork, and the rest remains a blur until my dessert-eating trance was broken by the *ching* sound of my weighty metal fork hitting the empty plate and I sank back to reality. I think my wife was finishing up some story or something. Shortly after I finished and was topped off with a final cup of coffee, the waiter appeared again with the check. As he set it down on the table, he said, "No hurry."

I opened the slender black folder, and the first thing I noticed was the price of my dessert: $18. My very first and only thought was, "Well worth it."

As I enjoyed that dessert, I was transported back to great memories from my childhood. I thought about my mom and brothers. So how do you get someone to gladly pay you $18 for a cookie? The answer is you earn it by giving that person more than just some hard, week-old, cellophane-wrapped cookie. You earn that person's business by creating value in the experience. One more question. Is anybody hungry for dessert right now?

A good illustration of how earning is a result of giving is how professional athletes are paid. Most of us are well aware of the highly publicized nine-figure contracts that professional athletes earn. I am confident that everybody understands that each athlete's contract is structured with details in place outlining terms, salary, and performance incentives, but like many others, I did not understand that many of them are paid by the game. Suspended? No game check. Injured off of the field and physically unable to perform? No game check. They do not feel like playing that day? No game check.

Like professional athletes, we are paid to show up and perform. Top agents understand that they get paid for what they have done, not for what they intend to do. Top agents show up, get out on the field, give it all they have got, and they earn it.

One of the last examples of how earning is a result of first giving is the law of reciprocity. Because our species is hard-wired to reciprocate behavior, it makes sense that by first giving to our clients we can then earn more business from them. Top agents always give their very best, give their clients all they need, give clients their ear and listen to their concerns, give more than they are obligated to and go the extra mile, to give them the very best experience. Giving is the key to earning. Giving purely, completely, and selflessly. So if earning is a direct result of giving, then what is it that top real estate professionals are out to earn?

A Sign of a Job Well Done

Referrals are not merely one person telling another person something like, "Hey, I know this dude named Sam or this chic named Sally; you should use them as your agent."

Referrals are 100 percent tied to what we discussed at the beginning of this chapter. Top agents understand that they must give to earn.

Whether they want to earn respect or make a personal connection or want to continue to earn someone's friendship, people must always give to earn. So when a top real estate agent gives great clients a wonderful and valuable experience, those good clients will want to share with others the experience that their agent gave them. Clients will want to give others the opportunity to have as great an experience as they had by working with their agent. It is a natural occurrence from a species whose survival is based deeply on sharing good things to want to share good experiences with those they know, love, and care about.

Another aspect is that people usually do business with people they identify with, people who are similar to them. This is no secret and has long been known. If agents take the time to go over a short list of past clients, they will see a pattern develop that many of the people they do business with are probably within a similar age range, or have similar family structures, have similar educational backgrounds, and likely share one or more relatable lifestyle attributes. More than likely an agent represents a close reflection of the referrers' character. Since it is said that "birds of a feather flock together," the chance that you will be referred to a friend, colleague, or family member of a past client who is both relatable to you as well as your past client is highly likely, when earning a referral. And that is a very good thing.

A word to the wise: steer clear of the appearance of offering to pay your past clients for referrals. In most cases blatantly offering to pay for a referral from someone who is not a licensed real estate agent is not allowed. To be clear, I am not saying not to reward them for referring business. What I am saying is to avoid creating some sort of quid pro quo scenario. We all have heard of pyramid-referral schemes, usually from big corporations in various industries on a national level. The truth is these scenarios, schemes, and situations, more often than not, generate leads, not referrals. True referrals must be earned and absolutely cannot be bought and paid for. Top agents know there is a clear and definitive difference between working with a referral client and a lead. Quite frankly, the difference is as clear as the difference between night and day. Boiled down to the essence, referrals are a transfer of trust from one person to another, and there is no good and lasting example of the capability of purchasing trust. It might fall into the category of brainwashing or some other psychological interplay, but true trust cannot be bought at any price.

Trust is Transferable but Not For Sale

As we clearly and emphatically established, trust cannot be bought; however, it can be transferred. A form of logical thinking called *modus ponens*, or the "if, then, therefore" model works something like this:

"I completely trust my friend Mary; my friend Mary completely trusts her top real estate agent, Anna; so because my friend Mary, whom I trust, also trusts her agent Anna, I can trust Anna too."

For illustrative purposes, I will explain it this way:

"*If* I completely trust Mary"

"and *then* I observe that Mary completely trusts her real estate agent, Anna,"

"*therefore* I can completely trust Anna to be my real estate agent too"

It is easy to understand that this is how most people work their way through life. As a matter of fact, odds are that the person reading this book right now is reading it as a result of this type of propositional logic.

Most people we come into contact with throughout the course of doing business have some clout, respect, or referral power with those within their own personal sphere of influence. Heck, to some extent, we all have influence over someone else in one way or another. But I want to discuss the outliers, particularly those who are pegged at the highest end of the spectrum. I label these people the super influencers. They are rare, but not hard to identify. Just look at the entries on Facebook for about five minutes, and you will come across at least one. They are in the know about everything, and people actually seek them out for their perspective or opinions. They are interesting creatures, and when top agents are in their good graces, they can be a geyser-like source of business. Word to the wise: super influencers' influence can cut both ways, meaning if a top agent steps out of bounds, delivers poor service, or in any way gets out of an influencer's good graces, it can be disastrous for the agent. Super influencers are valued for their opinions, and they protect themselves within their community, so do not screw it up. When working with referrals from a super influencer (and for that matter, everyone else), remember to always do what you say you are going to do and do it at the highest level. Never forget that you are probably not the only real estate agent that a super influencer knows and, for that matter, you are probably not the only real estate agent that most people know. With that fact in mind, never lose sight of the fact that you are one broken promise away from being replaced.

Mining for Gold

With the explosive popularity of reality television programs, we have all had the opportunity to learn a bit about every industry and hobby. Singers, dancers, musicians, people who perform home renovations or motorcycle customization—heck, there are even reality television shows about mixed martial arts and dermatologists who pop pimples. This relatively recent phenomenon of television entertainment genre has probably gotten its hooks into all of us through a show or two. For me it was a gold mining show. First off, I like money. More clearly, I like money because it is good for the good that it can do. So to me, the idea of finding money lying around in the dirt was intriguing. As well, I love to watch people who are willing to take a risk, work very hard, swing for the fences, and create the opportunity of acquiring vast riches. I am also a sucker for contraptions, especially those that have been around for centuries and function pretty much the same as they did two hundred years ago, so I have watched reality mining shows for the last few years and have enjoyed spending countless hours losing myself in the saga of a bunch of roughshod miners willing to take on the challenge of the Alaskan wilderness, weather, and pitfalls all while being followed around by large camera crews and production staff. You know, "reality." As an aside, I can picture a producer or director yelling out to the cast, "Don't mind us; pretend we are not here and just do what you do."

After watching countless episodes and becoming a seasoned armchair miner, I suddenly came to the realization that the steps that gold miners take to extract gold from the ground is very similar to what top real estate agents do to extract business. Although gold miners use the time-tested tools of the trade such as hoppers, trommels, pressurized water, shaker decks, and sluice boxes, top real estate agents do not use any of those things. However, the process miners use to separate the valuable gold flakes and nuggets from the tons and tons of pay dirt shares some common threads with the process that top real estate agents use in their operations. First, gold miners prospect for good ground. They search out a plot of land where they are likely to find gold. One of the processes that gold miners use is to drill test holes deep into the ground, extract the core of dirt, and pan it out to see if the paydirt bears enough gold to turn a profit. They lay these core holes in a grid pattern to map out the best path to follow to harvest the gold vein. But where the similarity of process is most noticeable is that when prospecting, the gold miners do not just randomly pick a spot. They look for areas that have the characteristics of gold-holding geography, which are usually located near areas that have produced gold before. And like gold miners, top real estate agents focus on areas that have produced business for them before, and the best area is near their past clients. While gold miners concentrate their efforts on areas with similar characteristics of those areas that have produced profitable gold for them in the past, there is no guarantee that the perfect plot of virgin ground is going to produce anything. And like gold miners, top real estate agents have no guarantee that each and every past client, referral partner, or influencer is going to produce more business. And top real estate agents, like gold miners, have no way of accurately predicting when the next shovel scoop will turn over the coveted glory lode, other than to *systematically* leave no good ground unturned. When you take a look at it, top real estate agents and gold miners' most commonly shared characteristic is being systematic, methodical, and persistent and employing a process that leaves no good ground unturned. Both miners and top agents show up, day in and day out, consistently slugging it out and putting in the hard work, knowing that eventually their efforts will produce gold.

Lack of Referral Business is a Warning Signal

The most frequently asked questions regarding referral business I get from agents who are newer to the real estate business, as well as a few that have been around awhile, is usually worded something like this: "Why is it that my clients just don't appreciate me?" and "Why don't past clients ever refer any business to me."

Whenever an agent asks these types of questions, or makes similar statements, I immediately know that there are only two possible reasons the potential rock star agent is experiencing this hardship. Either it is a result of reason number one, which is they are doing it all wrong, or it is reason number two, and they are not doing it at all. The "it" being referenced in both reasons is asking their past clients for referrals. When a good agent is not receiving referral business from past clients, it is always as a result of one of these two possibilities; hands down, without question, end of story. Whether an agent has been in the business for quite some time or if the ink on their real estate license is still wet, the lack of referral business is a result of never effectively asking for referrals or asking them in the wrong way. I am not necessarily concerned with the system that a real estate agent chooses to use. I am primarily concerned with the lack of value that they are creating for their past clients, referral partners, and sphere of influence as well as the recently met people they are looking to serve. Creating true value is always noticed, eventually. True value is always eventually rewarded, as well. It all boils down to the basics. If you are looking for people to serve for the sole purpose of serving only their real estate needs, you are doing it all wrong. Top real estate agents are always primarily laser-focused on serving people. If this message is not resonating with you, flip back a few pages to chapter three and start reading. Open your eyes and take a look around. I would bet that even with a minimal amount of creativity, any of you top real estate agents reading this book right now could find at least one person to serve within the next five minutes. Think back to chapter three and the section on who owes loyalty to whom. Remember, referrals are always earned, never just given.

One of the best overall indicators of the health of a real estate agent's business is referral volume. It is common for top real estate agents to spend literally zero dollars on brand-based marketing whatsoever and yet continually grow their business year after year by effectively focusing on referral-based business generation. The most notable strength of a referral-based business is that referrals have been proven to weather the storms and turbulence of volatility in the real estate market. When business is scarce, good people are always looking for top-performing professionals to serve them. And they usually find the most trustworthy professionals from—you guessed it—a referral from a trusted friend or family member. As well as generating a consistent stream of business, referrals are a controllable key driver when it comes to the health of your business. In fact, referrals are the most controllable source of business available. Top agents know this fact and leave nothing to chance when it comes to creating the right conditions to receive referral business. Top real estate agents find more and more clients to serve, because they are constantly providing value to others, consistently following up, and regularly staying in touch. Remember the profit is in the follow-up.

One of the aspects of the real estate business most often overlooked by agents is the aspect of total and complete real estate burnout. If you are new to the business of real estate sales and service, you might be thinking that you could never get burned out and that there is nothing that will ever quench the burning desire to serve those most in need of your professional guidance. Well, I thought that too. The most overlooked people in a top real estate agent's world are very rarely their clients, team members, colleagues, or family; most often it is themselves. I can tell you from years of observing, working with, and coaching top real estate agents that those who burned out the hardest and fastest were those who did not consistently and systematically generate referral business. Top agents know that by focusing on generating referral business they are not only focusing on taking care of the needs of those that they serve; they know they are taking care of themselves.

Ultimately, top agents know that if things are not going well and they are looking for someone to blame, they find a mirror, take a long look, and then get to work. That is not to say that we all could use more coaching, guidance, and mentoring; actually, far from it. But no one is ever going to seek you out, hold your hand, and rub your back while they ask how they can help you build your real estate practice. Look, if you are not creating a predictable and consistent referral business, you are to blame. That is the cold, hard truth. The bright side to that cold, hard truth is that when agents find that they are not consistently generating referral business, the problem is simple to correct. In addition to being simple to correct, the problem of low or no referral business usually can be turned around quickly, and the agent can be producing referral business almost immediately. If you find yourself starting out and wanting to get on the right track with referrals, or if you are stuck and the gift that should just keep on giving just ain't, here are a few things you should consider:

First of all, generating referrals should be your main source of real estate lead generation. Even if you are new to the business, this statement still applies. Perhaps you need to expand your thinking on the sources available to you to generate referrals or explore the best practices of top agents for creating a business where referrals come in like a tsunami. There are tons of resources, such as coaches, mentors, and colleagues that you can press into action. If your list of coaches and mentors is a bit short, consider reading *The Millionaire Real Estate Agent* and *Shift*, both by Gary Keller. Both books are full of strategies and tactics that I have found useful; you will not regret spending some time reading those books.

As well as considering your focus on generating referrals, also consider this: earning is a direct result of giving, so you might take some time to reflect on what it is that *you* are holding back. Do you need a mindset adjustment? Are you squarely focused on serving the people around you? Are you giving everyone you come in contact with the best of you? Another important consideration, and this applies across the business spectrum, is that one key predictor of success is directly related to how well you can get things done through others. One form of getting things done through others is most certainly generating referrals. Remember that generating referrals is a skill and skills can be learned, developed, and ultimately mastered.

People of Character Never Just Let You Win

Did any of you grow up in a competitive environment? Whether it was sibling competition, cousins, neighbors, or even parents and grandparents, any and all could have been competitive with you. Healthy and sporting competition is good for the soul. It is an inherently human trait. I remember sitting around at a lake cottage when I was young and watching the adults play cards. Even though it was always based on having fun and being a good sport, the competition was palpable as winning hands were smacked down onto the table and the victors gathered the cards and shuffled and called out the deal. Even the next day, the winners and losers verbally sparred about comebacks and winning streaks. The one thing I never remember was anyone just giving up, crying "uncle," and letting someone else win a cheap victory. As a matter of fact, I was raised to believe that letting someone win was considered a form of cheating. Without question, letting someone win was cheap, and "cheap victories ain't worth shit." True statement. So when I hear an agent say, even jokingly, "Hey, why don't you just give me some of your business to work?" it actually turns my stomach. Because after all, only losers would ever want a cheap victory. Referrals exist in the same realm. When you work for something and earn it, everybody feels great. Both for you and about themselves. When you show up and work to earn referrals on a consistent basis, people will want to see you earn that victory. However, many people will shy away from giving you a cheap victory. Why? Because it is cheating, and it ain't worth shit!

Top real estate agents also know, without a doubt, that there is zero luck involved in earning referrals. Simply put, it comes down to mathematics, pure and simple. Math has rules. The rules are that the more people that you effectively contact on a consistent and routine basis, the more referral business you will generate. You can take that statement to the bank. One thing for sure: you cannot predict when luck will show up, but through the use of proven systems and processes, coupled with diligent and consistent work ethic and drive, you can absolutely predict referral business.

People of Character Respect Diligent Work

Have you ever noticed how top producers and people of great accomplishment seem to rally around the newbies who get out, work hard, and strive to get results? Having had the advantage of working in a few different businesses across various industries, I have seen this scenario play out time and time again. There is a formula to it. First, it does not seem to matter if the new people show up as a new hire, promotion, or transfer. Often they are likeable, positive, confident, and eager. They are ambitious, hardworking, self-starters, and they are coachable, and then someone in a leadership position—such as a top salesperson or manager, CEO or boss—notices them and puffs them up and sets the expectation that they will succeed. The leaders create an air of success around them by the conversations they have about them, around them, and in front of them with other leaders in the organization. Some examples are statements like, "I'll tell you what, when Jane gets her first territory and gets off the sales bench, she is going to tear the cover off the ball" or "Peter, I can just see the winning oozing from every pore of your skin. You are going to crush it."

The newbies then grow into the perception that has been created around them. They have the character that makes them feel almost obligated to find a way to succeed, as if failure is not an option. Like magic, they go out and crush it. On a few occasions in my real estate brokerage, I have met a new associate and thought, "I can see it; she is going to be the next rookie of the year" or thought, "Man, he is going to crush it." I find myself energized by the person's energy, so much so, that I actually go out of my way to act as a resource to help in his or her pursuit of success. It is interesting how top real estate agents will go out of their way to mentor new agents who show up as go-getters. It also seems to spill out to those that they interact with as well.

When we humans witness one of our fellow brothers or sisters working hard, being self-disciplined and diligent and putting in hard work, we respect their efforts and drive. We want to share in the celebration of their success, not to take ownership of their success or claim to have been the reason for it, but to feel the energy from their success vicariously. It is clear to me that people who work to master any craft or discipline understand and appreciate all of the hard work achieving a high level of success requires, the hours of dedication and the self-control that the pursuit of mastery requires. It cannot be counterfeited, faked, or impersonated.

Generally speaking, people of all kinds want to see others succeed, especially those who are willing to work hard at it. A word of caution:

beware of those around you try to pull you down, hold you back, or in any way try to discourage you from reaching for the brass ring. It may not even be for nefarious reasons or ill intent. They may think they are trying to shield you from disappointment that they themselves may have experienced. If you find yourself surrounded by people who take steps to limit your potential or discourage your drive and ambition, vacate that environment immediately. The bottom line is that the majority of people want to see others around them reach the pinnacle of success, and often, those same people will go above and beyond to mentor, assist, or be a general guidepost for their success. This energy will wholly spill over and transmute into even more referrals.

I will share a situation with you that I experienced firsthand. Early in my career in real estate sales, I participated in an eight-week program where the goal was to jump-start a career and springboard forward by rapidly building a business pipeline through referrals. The instructor told us that we were going to participate in a contest, and we were to make phone calls to our sphere of influence and use this simple script: "Hello _____, this is _____, I was wondering if you could help me. I'm in a contest, and I want to win. Who do you know who might be looking to buy, sell, or invest in real estate now or in the future?"

To set the stage, I was a bit reluctant to make calls to my friends and colleagues to "bug" them for real estate referrals. I am sure that I am the only person who has ever felt this way when making these types of calls, so I do not expect you to be able to easily relate to my feelings of doubt (nudge, nudge; wink, wink). But I actually did something unusual for my patterned behavior. I embraced the uneasiness, and I made the calls. It was not easy. In the ten minutes allotted, I made only seven calls and left six messages. The magic happened on the seventh call. I connected with a friend of mine. She happened to serve on our town council, a fact that must had slipped my mind at the time, because if I had remembered that she served on town council, I probably would not have called her. You see, I also knew one of her fellow council members was in fact a top real estate agent. Truthfully speaking, if I had remembered, it might have been the only catalyst I needed to convince myself that she probably would not refer any business to me. I would have skipped it and moved on to the next phone number. I repeated the script verbatim and waited in silence for a few seconds, and those seconds actually seemed like an eternity. She replied, "Scott, funny that you called, because I just got a random inquiry today through my town council social media account from somebody named Jen from Oklahoma. She and her family are considering a move to the area and she asked if I could give her some guidance."

That one random action had a huge impact on the lives of all involved. Since reluctantly making that call so many years ago, Jen and her husband have become close family friends. Our families have vacationed together, and my wife and Jen have become close friends. I have camped, hiked, mountain biked, rafted, and coached youth athletics with her husband. Our youngest son and their oldest son are in the same grade and ended up in the same school and in the same class. They have play lacrosse together in the same league and at times on the same team in their lacrosse league and now play on the same high school varsity team. Our families have become true friends. Oh, and not only was I able to help them with their home purchase when they relocated to Colorado, but I also have helped them both directly and indirectly, through referrals, with no fewer than eight transactions.

As I write this, I am thinking of about a dozen other similar situations that have occurred throughout my real estate career that I could have cited. The moral of the story is that if you put in the work and push through the obstacles with the clear intent to serve others, great things will happen. If you do not believe me, I challenge you to prove me wrong.

Avoiding Reverse Referrals

Earlier I discussed the power of super influencers and the geyser-like affect that they can have on your business. I also warned that if you do not deliver the most impeccable service and customer care to the people that these super influencers send your way, their referrals will dry up fast. In that earlier example, because of your poor service, the super influencer just quit referring people; however, the case of a reverse referral is a bit different. See if you can spot the difference between a person who stops referring an agent to people and one who starts giving reverse referrals as you follow the conversation between two acquaintances below.

"Kate!?"

"Julie? My gosh, it's been so long since I've talked with you."

After catching up a bit, Julie asks, "Hey Kate, you and Steve just sold your house recently, didn't you?"

"Yeah, Julie, we did, and what a nightmare!"

Curious, Julie asks, "What, is the market that bad?"

"No," Kate quickly replies, "In fact, we received four offers and had a contract within two days of hitting the market. The problem was with our agent. All I can say is if you are thinking of selling your house, never work with _____."

Reverse referral scenarios play out multiple times a day all across the country. These reverse referrals are preventable in every case.

In politics, it is said that it is not the mistake that usually gets politicians in trouble, it is their attempt to cover up their mistake. It is the same spirit in basic customer service, and particularly in the real estate business, and it is usually not a mistake that will earn an agent a reverse referral; it is the lack of properly acknowledging and correcting a mistake that will. If I had to identify the singular issue that contributes most to the bad reputation that real estate agents undeservedly get today it would be rooted in these types of situations. Some real estate agents are terrible at delivering bad news. I believe that this is not exclusive to the profession of real estate sales itself, but it is magnified within our industry, because in general, real estate agents love people and seem to despise delivering less-than-optimal information to people. I firmly believe that it is rooted in the fact that most agents are people pleasers and also lack the skills to tactfully deliver unpleasant information. It may sound like a cop-out or that I am making excuses for abhorrent behavior, but far from it. What I am saying is that I do not believe that agents who are unwilling to address problems do so because they desire to deceive, misdirect, or harm their clients, but the exact opposite. They lack the capacity to hurt, let down, disappoint, or anger their clients and want to spare them the heartache and grief by trying to gloss over or fix a bad situation without involving their clients. Some agents think they are doing their clients a favor by attempting to avoid adding more stress to an already stressful situation. Again, I am in no way condoning this behavior. The mistake or bad news is usually easily remedied and is not the problem; it is the attempt to cover it up that causes all of the problems. In almost each class I teach to real estate agents I tell them same thing that I am going to tell you now. The only reason you are involved in the transaction is to be the professional advisor and voice of reason. Emotions have no place in the role you serve throughout the process of a real estate transaction. Your primary function is to present your clients with the facts so that they can then make fact-based decisions. Most of the time these bad-news situations arise from events that are out of the agent's control and the agent is only trying to save clients from additional stress. Withholding this information will always make the situation worse. Folks, I do not know how else to say it. Withholding information is blatantly lying to clients. Lying by omission is still a lie. Top real estate agents know there is only one way to handle situations, and that is honestly, transparently, and in a timely fashion. If you find being honest is too difficult a task, then respectfully I say you need to find another line of work. My apologies for being so harsh.

We as licensed real estate professionals have a duty to uphold. Most of us who are members of a real estate association have actually raised our right hand and taken an oath that we would uphold that duty. The best course of action is to acknowledge an issue, present it to the client, and then propose solutions to remedy the issue. Acknowledging the issue does not always mean taking blame. Most of the time these issues culminate from a succession of little twists and turns and then they end up in your lap like the hot potato. However, if agents drop the ball, they should admit it, apologize, and propose a remedy. As much as we all mistakenly think that these transactions belong to us as agents, we must remind ourselves that we are guiding our clients through *their* transactions, and by lying to them, by omission or otherwise, we are potentially damaging them, financially, emotionally, or even legally. Top agents conduct their business and guide their clients with the utmost skill and care, so take note. Top agents create systems and follow processes, and most of the time issues arise as a result of not following systems and processes to the letter. If agents find that they are constantly putting out fires, it is probably as a result of the lack of implementing and consistently following systems and process.

Even the agent who works with only one or two clients a month will find that without systems to rely on, simply taking a day off will result in many small fires or worse yet, a raging inferno. Run your life and business with a plan and by design, not merely by whatever random circumstance comes at you next.

It is important to consider that you may find yourself working with a client who refuses to be served. Whether they refuse to listen to your expert guidance or they choose to rely more on the advice of "a friend who is an agent" than your advice or they undermine your systems, processes, strategies, and models, it is up to you to choose whether you want to continue that business relationship. If you find yourself in a situation with a client who has unrealistic expectations or who refuses to follow any of your expert guidance, my experience is that the juice is never worth the squeeze. More often than not, those situations will result in reverse referrals, no matter how hard you work to serve those clients.

Train People to Send Quality Referrals

Once I had an agent ask me how I managed to get my past clients, sphere of influence, and strategic partners to send me high-quality referrals. I think he was expecting some long, drawn-out explanation involving complex systems, processes, mathematics, and some good old-fashioned voodoo. As he waited for my answer, I am pretty sure I saw a small bead of sweat forming on his forehead that was wrinkled and frozen in place along with his entire facial expression, from his toothy smile to his wide, unblinking eyes. I simply replied, "Well, I train them."

With the excitement one would expect at a turtle race, he replied, "Oh."

Which leads me to the next point of business, which is how do you train people to send you high-quality referrals? Simply put, I tell past clients exactly what they should do whenever they come across someone they think I should meet with. How that system works for each agent is as unique as a thumbprint. Some agents prefer that their past clients text the person's name and contact information; others hand out stacks of cards to their past clients for distribution whenever necessary; still others have a referral page on their website. My answer to you is whatever works best for you, with one single caveat. You must implement a simple and easy process and then train your clients, friends, partners, and whoever else will send referral business, and then do it the same way every time.

What are the key takeaways for creating your system? Again, a consistent, simple, easy system that you train people to use. Agents tend to complicate things such as this. Do not do that. Here is an example of just how easy an effective referral system can be to implement. The next time you are on the phone with a person you think might be able to refer some clients to you, wrap your phone call up using this simple script:

"Well Pete, it was great catching up with you, and I am looking forward to seeing you and your wife at the football tailgates again this fall. Hey, before I let you go, can I ask you a favor?"

They always say, "Yes."

"I know in your line of work that you come in contact with a lot of people. The next time one of those people mentions real estate, would you mind texting me their name and telephone number with a few words about if they are looking to buy or sell?"

They always say, "Sure."

"Thanks a lot. Talk soon, bye." Click.

Make a habit of training the people who refer business exactly how to refer you business. Over time you will develop a network of people who send you texts like the following:

Bill Smith
(123) 555-6789
Wants to list his house, I told him about you, call him.

By creating a simple path to connect and telling people exactly how to make the connection, you will be training a small army of advocates on exactly how to send you more great people to serve.

The final piece of the equation of how to train people to send you high-quality referrals rests squarely on your shoulders. Acknowledge and reward the people who go out of their way to refer high-quality prospects to you. It is critical that you immediately reward those who send you referrals and then always follow up promptly, professionally, and persistently with anyone they refer to you until you are able to make contact. There is no greater kiss of death that will end a referral relationship than not following up and contacting the person who has been referred to you. Do I need to elaborate, or do you understand? You understand? Good. Let's move on.

Use the Force (Multipliers)

You must work to establish a solid relationship with super influencers, because they are force multipliers. This is not about leg-humping and begging an influencer to send business your way; in fact it is quite the opposite. It is about building a relationship with them and connecting with them through what you share in common. Whether it is through shared relationships with others in the community, common interests and hobbies, being members of the same organization, or that your kids attend the same school, be seen and make the connection. I wish there was some sort of magic button for this, but there is not. What it will take is good old-fashioned politicking, pressing the flesh, and making beneficial introductions over time. Other agents are also great force multipliers. Building solid referral networks of agents across your state, region, country, and the globe is a never-ending pursuit for top agents. Top real estate agents are always looking for connections with other top agents they can trust to take care of referral clients at a level equal to or greater than the level of service they themselves provide.

Even top agents have been burned by making a referral to a less-than-professional agent. More important than the lost referral fee is the loss of trust from someone you have worked so hard to serve at a high level. When it comes down to crunch time, you want to know with absolute certainty that you are handing off the care of your clients' referral to capable hands.

Another effective strategy is to build a collection of professional endorsements from people outside of the real estate business, especially those you have referred business to. Endorsements from title company representatives, lenders, carpet installers, contractors, automobile dealers, and any other countless people that you refer business to will go a long way in building your credibility. Be selective in who you choose to align yourself with, because in this case, your reputation is connected to theirs and theirs is connected to yours. Take the time to follow up with the people you refer to the professionals you have aligned with. Make certain the people that you refer are receiving the high level of care and customer service you assume they are receiving. When it comes to your reputation, do not take the chance of aligning yourself with someone who says one thing yet operates completely differently.

Earning Referrals and a Marathon Mindset

A marathon, if you are not aware, is a race of a distance of 26.2 miles. Statistically speaking, most people who start a marathon and quit before finishing do so in the twentieth mile. I find this statistic interesting. Not mile five or mile ten or even mile fifteen, but mile twenty. Why? I mean, that is more than 75 percent of the way through the entire distance. I am sure that sports psychologists have studied this phenomenon, but it is mind boggling that a runner would make it more than 75 percent of the way through such a grueling undertaking only to give up so near the end. With that little tidbit in mind, it is important that you understand that earning referrals is similar to running a marathon. Many agents who quit trying to build their referral business do so after putting in most of the effort and hard work, but before they start reaping all of the wonderful rewards of a referral-based business. One of the key ingredients to building a strong, referral-based real estate business is time. Top agents know that having patience cannot be overlooked when nurturing and building a referral network. The adage that "Rome wasn't built in a day" is often used, but to that I say, "Yeah, but I bet the shitty parts of Rome probably were." All joking aside, building anything that will stand the test of time, including a referral-based real estate business, requires a solid plan that is implemented consistently and at a high level over time.

I seem to be full of adages, so here is another one that applies to building a referral-based business: "a watched pot never boils." If you have ever been hungry and waited and waited by the stove for your macaroni water to boil, you can relate. When it comes to measuring success early on in your career, focus on doing the referral-generating activities of a top real estate agent and not the results. You may create some luck early on and start receiving referrals right away. However, most likely you will spend a lot of time nurturing and growing your referral business before you receive any referral business. Be patient, persistent, and professional. It is said that "If you build it, they will come," so start building.

It's Always Been a Matter of Trust

Referrals done right allow for a seamless transfer of trust from one person to another with no erosion of that trust. At the beginning of this chapter I laid out the simple formula where I trust Mary; Mary trusts her agent, Anna; therefore I trust Anna too. This formula is the basis of all referrals. Referrals are simply a transfer of trust. Top real estate agents know that their only product is great customer service, and in turn, great customer service is possible only through the development and use of great systems and processes. The foundation of a strong and lasting referral-based real estate business boils down to how affectively you build your systems and processes and how rigorously and methodically you follow them, not just for systematizing referrals but systematizing everything that you do.

9

Processes and Systems are Your Only Product

Real estate agents do not sell a tangible product. Shocker! Real estate agents do not sell hamburgers, hammers, honey, hot pants, horseshoes, or helium balloons. I will even go so far as to say that (gasp) strictly speaking, our product is not houses, because houses are the product of home builders, and the last I checked, none of the top real estate agents I know build houses. Sure, the argument can be made that an agent's product is the marketing of houses, but that is not true either. After all, a real estate agent's product is not the multiple listing service or brochures. I once heard a real estate agent trainer say that our primary job is to sell ourselves. Hell, that joke writes itself. If you have been around this business long enough, like five minutes long, you might argue that many agents do have a lot in common with prostitutes in the way they conduct business. They just hang out, show off the goods with a great glamour shot or witty pickup line, and do amazing tricks. Before I take this all a bit too far, if I haven't already, I stand by the title of this chapter. Top real estate agents know that the only products that they have to offer to clients are their processes and systems.

Now that you know where I stand on the subject of the valuable products we agents offer, let's take a dive into how our only products—our systems and processes—set us apart and establish our unique selling proposition. How you conduct business will be apparent by how you conduct your initial meeting with a client. Whether you are conducting a buyer consultation or you are meeting with prospective listing clients at their home, your systems and processes will be on full display. The initial meeting for a buyer or seller will follow processes that you have established, tweaked, and documented and then follow the same way each time you make a presentation. This first professional interaction will set the tone for how you conduct business. Are you polished, succinct, clear, and organized, or do you just wing it every time? Believe it or not, you are auditioning to serve your prospective clients in a role as their representing agent. Do you know your script? Do you even have one? Sadly, many agents who have been conducting business for years have never taken the time to memorize their lines for this critical audition. Being prepared is a habit, and so is not being prepared. How do you "show up" in the eyes of your potential client? Take this opportunity to take control and set the tone for how you conduct business as a professional real estate agent. As well, the initial meeting is the perfect opportunity to establish the boundaries and guidelines under which you operate. Set the expectations up front and assertively by clearly outlining your business hours, when you return phone calls and emails, and when they will receive updates and progress reports, such as weekly or biweekly calls to discuss showing activity, feedback, and market-condition reports. Your processes and systems will showcase that you and your team members are effective at communication. The National Association of Realtors® has conducted multiple studies that clearly illustrate that among the top reasons clients are dissatisfied with the service that their real estate agent provided was lack of communication. Yes, the "dog and pony show" matters. The solid processes that you employ at the initial consultation will absolutely set the tone for how you conduct yourself as a professional and is the one shot for you to showcase the only products you have to offer: your systems and processes. The transaction itself is a collection of processes within multiple systems, from title and escrow, showing management, lender preapprovals, and closings and consists of a ton of moving parts. What message does your initial consultation convey about the processes that you use to conduct business? It is the first glimpse that a prospective client will get of your only products, the first experience with your systems and processes.

What is a process? At a basic level, a process is a standardized succession of documented steps. Simple, right? The concept of processes is pretty simple to grasp. The two key words are *standardized* and *documented*.

Standardized means *the same every time,* and *documented* means *in writing*. For any business activity to be considered a process, it must be both in writing and completed the same way every time. Top real estate agents understand that if a multi-step task within their business is not in writing and completed the same way every time, they are just winging it. Processes allow top real estate agents the ease of following steps and tracking milestones along the way of a transaction. Processes also allow everybody who is part of the team conducting the transaction to stay in the loop. Processes are the tools that keep everyone on the same page to clearly manage the transaction and to know exactly what has been completed and what needs attention. Highly refined and documented processes are easily assignable and allow a multitude of people to track and follow the progress of the transaction with little to no direction beyond the initial training they received.

You might be wondering, "Well, Scott, what is the difference between a system and a process?" At that point I'd respond, "I am so glad that you asked."

Up to this point we have established that a process is a clearly documented collection of steps. A system is then a collection of processes. Again, simple. It must be composed of two elements to be an actual system; it must be standardized, and it must be documented in writing. Top real estate agents may have dozens of systems made up of hundreds of processes. For the sake of an example, let's say that a real estate agent has an administrator whose primary job is to answer the phone. A call comes in, and that administrator has a process to follow when answering the phone. Maybe a greeting like, "Hello, John Smith Home Team. This is Joe. How may I help you today?"

The caller says he is looking for more information about a home that the John Smith Home Team has listed. The administrator has another process, "Well, thank you for your call. Yes, I have received a few calls about that listing at one two three Main Street. If you will give me a second, I will look it up in our system. While I have you here, I see you are calling from (234)-555-6789. Is this a cell phone or land line?"

Caller responds, "It's a land line."

Joe continues, "A land line. Good. Got it. Also, what is the best email for you, so I can send you this listing information?"

The caller gives Joe his email address, and Joe replies, "Great. Got it."

The caller then asks if he and his wife could have a showing of the property. There happens to be a process for when a sign caller would like to view a property as well. The administrator asks, "I think John is in the office, and I am sure that he can make that happen for you and your wife. I can see he is not currently on the phone. If you hold a second, I will immediately transfer you over to him."

This collection of processes is the John Smith Home Team's system for handling inbound sales calls.

Notice that I said that this is the John Smith Home Team's system for handling inbound sales calls. I did not say that this is the inbound sales call system that you or your team should use. Anyone could use this system, but it must fit your specific needs or the specific needs of your team. It is not the case that one size fits all when it comes to implementing processes and systems. The processes and systems in use by top real estate agents are as numerous as the number of agents in the marketplace. The truth of the matter is that individual real estate agents and real estate teams and all group structures in between can and do use vastly different and unique processes and systems to achieve the same goals—to serve their people at the highest and best level possible.

The processes and systems that teams and agents create are largely dependent on their businesses overall mission, vision, and values. A great analogy is that of taking a cross-country road trip from New York City to San Francisco. There are literally hundreds of unique routes one could travel. Depending on the travelers' individual goals and objectives, whether they want to stop in their hometown to visit along the way or they would like to swing through the little town where they went to college or stop off to see the world's largest concrete egg in Mentone, Indiana, each route would be vastly different.

Let's take a moment to talk about doing a little R&D in the realm of processes and systems. By R&D I mean Rip off & Duplicate. The fact that the processes and systems we put in place will be as unique and as individualized as each of us are does not prevent us from borrowing and adapting other top real estate agent's processes and systems to make them our own. Hey, success leaves clues, so follow them and do not attempt to reinvent the wheel. Maybe you have observed other real estate agents' models in action, and you admire how they do business. There is nothing wrong with emulating their examples. Other real estate agents' success can be used as a guide, but just remember, never lose sight of who you are and what makes you unique. From your mission to your values to your overall vision, to be a top real estate agent, you have an identity, and that identity should be incorporated into your process and systems.

Throughout the years I have heard many versions of the same arguments and excuses when it comes to concisely documenting, implementing, and following processes and systems in the real estate business: "I am just a single agent; why should I waste my time on building out processes?" or "Every transaction and client is different, so why should I create an environment that might be constraining to me or my client?"

A great illustration of why top agents use solid, documented, and repeatable processes and systems comes in the same form as a FedEx commercial that aired a few years ago. In the commercial a group of three businesspeople are heading to a meeting. One of the characters asks the boss where his presentation is. He replies, "It's all up here," and as he points to his head in a display of confidence, he turns the corner in a cubicle farm and runs smack dab head first into an open filing cabinet drawer and gets knocked out. Unshaken, the two remaining businesspeople continue their brisk walk to the high-stakes meeting, and the woman says to the other guy, "So do you have the presentation?" With the utmost confidence he replies, "Yep, I'm John's backup. Everything he knew, I know." They cut through what appears to be a break room, and the second guy slips, falls, lands flat on his back, and knocks himself out as well. The commercial ends with the woman standing in the conference room in front of a dozen or so people without a clue of the presentation she is supposed to present. Regardless of the marketing message the delivery company was trying to convey, the executive's attitudes were what I noticed most. The bottom line is that without well-thought-out documented processes and systems, all you are left with is a collection of thoughts, with no rhyme or reason, and no contingency plan other than to just wing it. The bottom line is such a setup cannot be followed by you or your team.

If you are a single agent, I have some news for you. As a single agent, you still have a team. It is made up of all the people involved in the transactions you represent, such as your recommended home inspectors, title and escrow officers, mortgage lenders, your brokerage team responsible for collecting and archiving your transactional records, your stager, your handyman/woman and whoever else you come into contact with throughout the course of completing a transaction. They are all on your team. With so much activity simultaneously taking place throughout the course of each individual transaction and with so many moving pieces, why would you choose to just wing it? How do each of your individual clients prefer to be contacted, how do you go about sending the signed purchase agreement to the title company to start the title process, or how do you get your clients in contact with two or three home inspectors to choose from? Without the slightest, most basic documentation of the processes and systems that drive your business, how in the world could you ever leave town on an enjoyable, relaxing vacation? An even more sobering thought is this: how could you ever leave town on a moment's notice for an emergency or family matter?

It makes no difference whether you are an army of one or you have a team of dozens, vague instructions and text messages leave too much open to interpretation, and folks, that ain't good. Simply put, when there are not concise processes and systems, documented and followed the same way each and every transaction, you will find yourself in situations that lead to unpredictable creativity. When agents exist in an environment of constant unpredictability, items are overlooked, deadlines are missed, balls get dropped, and clients are disappointed. Top agents know that to produce consistent predictable results, they must operate within a consistent and predictable environment. Top agents also know that there is no such thing as a naturally occurring consistently predictable environment in the realm of real estate sales. Top agents know that in the world we operate in, a consistently predictable environment is not going to magically manifest out of thin air. Top agents know they must create processes and systems to ensure a consistently predictable environment. Without concise processes and systems that are clearly documented and consistently followed, there can be little to no accountability. Top agents know that if there are not clear instructions outlining the exact who, what, and when, there will only be excuses, blame, and failure.

If it has not occurred to you yet, great processes and systems create an environment of predictability. Top agents know that easy-to-follow, documented processes and systems must create predictability, or they are weak and virtually useless. It may seem obvious that the best systems are simple, but it is easy to get distracted with complex, over-thought processes. Keep it simple and reduce each process and system to the most basic form, with just enough information and guidance that a seventh grader could follow along. Top agents know that great processes and systems should eliminate complexity and uncertainty, not create it.

One of the trends in the real estate business today, and I believe it to be a good one, is that of using some leverage and outsourcing some of your processes and systems. There are countless systems and countless lead generation vendors out there, too many to shake a stick at. Rather than diving head first into the twisting and turning world of real estate system vendors that are available today, I will focus in on one: the transaction coordinator.

Each market and each state requires unique processes and systems when speaking from a transactional standpoint. As they say, all real estate is local, so be sure you are in compliance with your state and local licensing board and meet the requirements of a transaction co-ordinator being licensed or not and the legalese surrounding this type of business structure. Taking the first step of outsourcing your trans-action coordination can be a leveraging miracle, if you approach it the right way. Top agents understand that when hiring a third-party transaction coordinator, they must find a professional that has an approach to doing business similar to their own. There must be some basic chemistry at play, or the agents and their transaction coordinators might be at each other's throats. When you are outsourcing the paper-pushing portion of a transaction, understand that clearly defined and documented expectations and benchmarks are not an option; they are a necessity. The most critical of these is how and when the transaction coordinator will be communicating with you, with your clients, with the title and escrow team, and with your inspectors. Virtually every bit of communication must be clearly laid out up front. As well, the transaction coordinator's communication style should mirror the communication style you use with your clients, partners, and team members. One of the biggest mistakes that agents make when outsourcing this portion of their business is that they also outsource all the communication as well. Do not lose control of the communication with your clients. We are just briefly scratching the surface on outsourcing, just understand that the buck stops at your desk, because you can outsource the activity, but you cannot outsource the responsibility. The responsibility for every outcome rests solely on your shoulders, and you must inspect the results that you expect from everyone that you are in business with, especially when they have so much interaction with your clients. When executed well, utilizing a transaction coordinator can be a wonderful experience that delivers an ultra-high customer experience to your clients, and when done poorly, your outsourcing efforts will backfire and result in missed deadlines, delayed closings, and disappearing clients.

Everyone Respects Effective Processes and Systems

Well-thought-out, documented, organized, and tightly followed processes and systems will showcase your business and prove you are an organized and detail-oriented real estate professional. This is likely the single biggest transaction that most people complete in their lifetimes, and having a competent, organized professional at the helm brings peace of mind to clients. Your processes and systems set the tone for how you do business. Top agents know that if they appear to be disorganized or less than on top of it all, their clients will go elsewhere in search of a real estate professional. Most of all, solid and well-implemented processes and systems provide clients and partners with a sense of relief that details will be handled, deadlines will be met, i's will be dotted, and t's will be crossed. Top agents understand that the way that clients view the agent's processes and systems is directly connected to how clients will view the agent. Perception is reality, and if clients perceive that details might fall through the cracks, clients might leave for greener pastures and seek out a more professional real estate agent.

Processes and Systems Are the Path to Mastery

Have you ever played a game of billiards? You know, pool? Whether you are a novice like me or a hustler like Minnesota Fats, you understand the basic premise of the game; use a pool cue to strike the white cue ball to then strike one or more of your balls to systematically knock all of your balls into one of the six pockets in the corners and center long side of a rectangular green table and be the first player to clear the table of all of your balls, and then last, the black eight ball. Each time you make a shot into one of the pockets, your turn will continue until you fail to get a ball into a pocket, at which time your opponent then has a turn. In order to knock all of your balls into the pockets before your opponent, the best strategy is to optimally string together the best sequence for hitting the balls and to leave the cue ball in a great position each time for the next shot. Sometimes it requires that you pass up a very easy shot and take a harder one that will leave the cue ball better positioned for the next shot. Pool players like me refer to this strategy as thinking two or three shots ahead. Just like the best pool players and chess players, top real estate agents know that solid and structured processes and systems allow them to anticipate three steps ahead. Superb processes and systems allow agents to get out ahead of potential problems, anticipate solutions, and remain a few steps ahead. When you can do that as a real estate agent, you will master the common as well as the less common situations that have the potential to derail a transaction. Another way that processes and systems pave the path to mastery is that they are repetitive, and repetition is the mother of all skill. Think of the pursuit of mastery that professional athletes take. Most world-class athletes have spent a lifetime developing muscle memory to operate in high-stress situations in a near automatic state. Just like world-class athletes, top real estate agents know they often operate in high-stress situations, and when their processes and systems are ingrained into their daily habits, they can respond to nearly any situation with near automatic precision to move the transaction forward.

Processes and systems also serve as the roadmap to get to the WIN: What's Important Now. Just like the earlier example of taking the right shots in the right sequence in the game of pool, mastery comes to agents who understand how to avoid the minutia and focus on the most important priority at the moment. Top agents use their processes and systems to strategically take shots in the right order to deliver winning results.

Often in the midst of chaos the training kicks in. In military engagements, when things go sideways, the countless hours of repetition, physical training, live-fire drills, and overall focus on discipline kicks in and gives soldiers the wherewithal to operate within a structure in the middle of pure chaos. Within the real estate world, albeit to a much lesser extent than in a battle, real estate transactions often present a high degree of variables wrapped up in situations that require quick decisions and precision responses. When operating within such situations daily, having a solid plan is key. Top real estate agents know their processes and systems and know they can fall back on their processes and systems when things get intense. Sometimes in the heat of battle, in keeping with the military theme, details get missed and the ball is sometimes dropped. With solid processes and systems in place, top agents can quickly identify and correct most problems. As the adage goes, "It is what you don't know that will kill you."

Processes and Systems Serve as a Benchmark

Documented processes and systems provide a tangible, viewable form of a transaction. After the fact, postmortem, in a debriefing—however you would like to say it—top real estate agents know that processes and systems expose weaknesses and highlight exactly where a breakdown occurred. This information allows top agents to identify exactly what parts of their processes need to be addressed and corrected. Well implemented processes and systems allow you to discover patterns and shortcomings within the systems. In a way, well-run systems are self-correcting. If and when bottlenecks and issues arise, they are easily identifiable and in turn easily correctable. Well-implemented processes and systems also allow agents to easily compare and contrast their systems with other top professionals' systems to identify ways to make improvements, change or streamline their current processes and systems, and make them even more efficient.

Well-implemented processes and systems also bring peace of mind, in that they allow an agent to see a snapshot of multiple transactions in real time with an up-to-the-moment status on all fronts and of all the actions that are taking place simultaneously. Top agents use their processes and systems to identify potential soft spots and address any of these items before they arise and derail or delay a transaction. Overall, the processes and systems that you develop will allow you to accurately measure, evaluate, and improve your overall performance of your day-to-day business operations.

A key question to ask yourself when designing, implementing, and following great systems comes down to this: are my processes and systems scalable? To put it another way, will my systems work as well at my current sales volume as they would if I tripled my business? Another consideration to make is if your current systems allow for the growth and expansion of your business necessary to achieve your long-term business goals, or whether these systems be easily adapted to changing market conditions or expanding or contracting business environments. Top agents take all these thoughts into careful consideration. Implementing as many scalable processes and systems from the get-go will save you and your team from having to learn and re-learn new processes and systems as your business grows, markets change, and business conditions fluctuate. In the long run, a little upfront planning will go a long way in saving both time and money.

Are You Building a Business, or Do You Just Have a Hobby?

This chapter outlines the basics of processes and systems. We have explored many aspects and benefits of structuring your real estate practice around solid processes and systems. We have discussed how implementing strong processes and systems fosters an environment of accountability and allows top real estate agents to inspect their business activities and compare those with the results they expect. In closing this chapter, I would like to touch on arguably the most important takeaway. Processes and systems are your only product. I firmly stand by that idea. To look at it another way, if you agree with me that process and systems are the only products you can offer a client, then by choosing not to implement solid, documented, and concise processes and systems, your real estate practice is nothing but a mere hobby. Top real estate agents know that they owe their clients, partners, and the public they serve their very best. When agent's half-ass their processes and shoot from the hip, it shows. Other real estate professionals, as well as prospective clients, can easily see through flimsy real estate agents with no standards of operation. It is easy to pick out those agents who are out there just chasing commissions with no long-term focus on their client's future real estate needs and overall goals. Perception makes reality, and when an agent just wings it, their outcomes are lackluster, and the reality of that approach will result in very short career in real estate.

10

The Power of Force Multipliers and Strategic Alliances

No one succeeds alone—ever. To be clear, I am not questioning the fact that if you are in the business of real estate, you are a self-starter. It was you who got up the courage to start asking questions or searching online for the qualifications that your state requires for real estate licensing. You pushed through the dark days that came in the beginning of your career, going weeks or months without a paycheck to show for all of your hard work. Perhaps you are at that point as you read this. You held all the open houses and did the door knocking, the prospecting, made the phone calls and contacts, and yes, it was you who walked two miles uphill (both ways) just to put the umpteenth open house sign out in a blizzard. If I have not been clear thus far, I believe that real estate agents are, without a doubt, absolutely singularly responsible for their career success. We few weary souls forged our own path and staked our claim to our hard-fought career in real estate sales.

What I am discussing here is that on top of being a self-starter, you must be great at getting things done through others. Without question, the number-one job of a real estate agent is to generate business. Some may question this fact, but I do not. Gary Keller wrote in *The Millionaire Real Estate Agent* that you can be the greatest negotiator on planet earth, you can know each and every line of the purchase contract like the back of your hand, and you can be a real estate sales marketing genius, but without a client to serve, all those skills mean nothing.

If a real estate agent's first duty is to generate leads (read *business*), then the more efficiently you can accomplish that foundational task, the more successful you will be at serving buyers and sellers who desperately need your skills. Top real estate agents understand that in the game of lead generation there is a lot of ground to cover, and they also know that they absolutely do not need to do it alone. There is zero nobility in real estate martyrdom. You must realize that delegating is at the heart of your chosen profession in real estate sales. You can get your hands on a lot of resources, but the most precious of all is time, and time is finite, limited, and irreplacable.

Recognize Your Biggest Limitation Is Time

One of the adages I heard early on in my career, and one of many that turned out to be so very true, is that if you do not learn how to effectively "run" your business, then your business will surely "run" you. We all know that there are only twenty-four hours in a day, and we have no problem understanding that simple fact. As we discussed in chapter five, the highest form of serving others is, from day one, to clearly set the expectations of how you conduct business and then adhere to and exceed those expectations. Top real estate agents conduct business this way without fail. I get it that when you are a new agent and you are working floor duty and someone calls while sitting in a car out front of a listed home and wants to see it now, well, giddy up! You are out the door and in your car in a flash. This is what I call being a pop tart. While this is the reality of an agent eager to earn clients and successfully guide them to the closing table, it is a dangerous precedent to set with a client. Being a pop-tart type of agent who pops up at every whim of a client, an agent who answers the phone at all hours and who sets no boundaries, is a recipe for burnout. With that said, the biggest opportunity to burn yourself out, by far, is going it alone. Let's take a look at what top real estate agents do to build and leverage strategic alliances and force multipliers in the area of generating business.

What Is a Strategic Alliance?

A strategic alliance is a business-to-business bilateral referral relationship with other business owners and their staff. The idea is simple. Top real estate agents seek out people in complementary businesses, start relationships, and then pass referrals back and forth, creating a mutually beneficial business arrangement with people they have gotten to know, both in character and their business practices. When I say "complementary" businesses, the first types of business people who come to mind are the usual suspects: home inspectors, insurance agents, painters, carpet cleaners, movers, handymen/women, contractors, landscapers, and every other trade or service associated with either improving or maintaining a home. But I am here to tell you from firsthand experience that top real estate agents need to cast their net much, much wider. I have had clients ask me for referrals to veterinarians, auto mechanics, youth sports organizations, personal trainers, cattle ranchers, artists, car dealers, furniture stores, fishing guides, and just about every other out-of-the-ordinary request you can imagine. I once had a client ask me for a referral to an equine trainer. These requests are particularly common with relocation clients who have no local connections whatsoever. The more solid relationships that you seek out and maintain, the more of a valuable resource you will be to your clients. And the more solid relationships you seek out and maintain with top-notch professionals and service providers will result in more referral business, guaranteed. Well, almost guaranteed, depending on how you approach it. This all sounds great, right? Well, then how does one conjure up such powerful relationships with like-minded business owners? Let's discuss a few techniques that top real estate agents use to build a solid strategic alliance referral network.

The absolute no-brainer first step is to take some time and identify the people you already know who are referring business and businesspeople within your personal sphere of influence that might be a good fit as strategic partners. You may know several dozen or you may not know any, depending on how deep and wide your sphere of influence is. Nonetheless, take the time to scour your memory and the contact list in your phone and compile a list of potential referral partners that you think might be a good fit. Once you have arranged your list and narrowed it down, it is time to get purposeful in building a solid, results-producing strategic alliance network.

Strategic Alliance Relationship Starters

To sum it up in a sentence, a strategic alliance relationship starter is nothing more than a business-to-business contact or meeting with the purpose of creating a mutually beneficial business-referral relationship with another business owner or service provider in the area where you conduct your real estate business. I am sure that the full scope of this concept seems fairly clear so far; however, there are agents who make costly mistakes at this point, particularly with who they choose to get into a referral relationship with and how they screen these business owners to discover if the relationship is a good fit, both in the business owner's approach to customer service and overall competency in their given trade, profession, or service.

Even when it comes to businesspeople within your sphere of influence, it is critically important that you stay true to the process and follow the most basic of screening steps; otherwise your clients will end up with poor service that *you* recommended. And more commonly, you will end up in a one-way referral relationship where you are sending considerable amounts of business, but as far as referrals coming back your way, it is mostly silence (cue the chirping crickets).

We have already discussed identifying and making a list the businesspeople already within your network, but what about building your network? Once you have completed the exercise of going through your contact list and network of business owners you know, it is time to identify businesses and businesspeople you do not yet know but suspect would be a good partner to be in a referral relationship with. Top real estate agents know many of the service providers in their given market area, and they are always looking for more. Some great resources that are easily available and are nearly all free are local advertising mailer packets (you know, the thick envelope that shows up in your mailbox with dozens of coupons from local business owners). These direct-mail coupon packets are a great resource because they illustrate that these business owners have a couple of great traits. One, they clearly would like to grow their businesses, and two, they are willing to be proactive by marketing and advertising to do so. Another element to take into consideration is that the business owners that use such marketing strategies are usually not the usual "top of mind" type of businesses. They typically comprise newer and growing business that are in the expansion mode, seeking a bigger customer base to serve (just like you). Another great resource available to most real estate professionals is to simply tap into your overall network of people, your sphere of influence, your friends, colleagues, and family and ask what great service providers they know that you should know. Your message could be as simple as this: "Hey, I have some clients that may be looking for a plumber (fill in the blank with whatever trade or multiple trades you are targeting) in the future, and I was wondering who you might know who handles your plumbing projects."

This is a great method to kill two birds with one stone, because it could also be a lead generation call as well by finishing up with, "Before I let you go, who do you know that might be considering buying or selling a home?"

Agents have also used social media to ask business referral questions as well, but a word of caution. Do not skip the phone call step. If you use social media to ask a blanket question about recommended service providers, be sure to follow up with people on the phone or through text or instant messaging to thank them and ask for permission to reach out. When people refer a service provider or business owner to you, always thank them and ask something like this: "Thank you for the name of (their plumber). Is it okay if I tell them you referred me to them?" This extra effort turns a cold call into a warm referral call, which is nice.

Some other resources that top agents use to find high-quality service providers are local business association member lists, local youth sports team or league sponsors, business advertisements on the sides of vehicles, phone directories, websites and internet banner ads, and whatever other resources that they can think of. The important takeaway is that top agents know that to build a strong alliance of high-quality service providers, they need to be on the lookout for new partners continually. Face it; business is in constant flux. People move, switch careers, open new businesses, close businesses, and retire. In addition, markets ebb and flow. Business is in constant motion, and top agents always keep their pipeline full.

After going through the process of searching out and identifying high-quality service providers, you should have a very sizable list. Now that you have identified businesspeople you may already know; businesspeople that your friends, family, and collogues may know; and businesspeople you have not met yet, it is time to reach out and get to know them better.

At this point top real estate agents start smiling and dialing to get in touch with the list of potential referral partners. The success rate to convert your calls to appointments will be the most challenging with those you are cold calling. Those that were referred to you by your wider network will agree to meet with you at a much higher rate than the cold calls. You will probably find that you will have a near 100 percent conversion to an appointment with those you already have some sort of a relationship with. Do not overcomplicate these calls. Your message should be nothing more than, "Hey, I saw your advertisement in the coupon book last week, and it seems that you and I are both looking to grow our businesses. I would like to learn more about your business, and I may have some business referrals to send to you. Do you have fifteen or twenty minutes on Tuesday morning or Thursday morning to meet me for a cup of coffee?"

There are a few things that you should be paying attention to during these calls. How do they answer the phone, are they professional, did a receptionist answer for them? What was the overall experience that you had on the phone when contacting the company? Chances are very good that whatever you experienced, anyone that you refer to them will experience as well. This call is the initial screening tool to help you decide if you would like to be in a referral relationship with them.

Once you secure the appointment and you actually meet, what were your impressions of their professionalism and demeanor? This goes for businesspeople already in your network too. Do they appear professional in public, are they on time, did they shake your hand or otherwise greet you? Remember, you are really just conducting pre-interviews for future referrals. Do they have processes and systems in place, or do they just wing it? These are very important indicators that can help you decide if you want your business associated with a business like theirs.

When you sit down, be sure that you exchange contact information. Delve into the basics of how long they have been in business, how many employees they have or would like to have, what their target for growth for this year and next year are, and what are any challenges they are currently facing in their business. Spend the first five minutes listening to them and getting to know a bit about them. If you still feel like they might be a good referral fit with your real estate practice, lay out exactly what you are looking for with something like, "You mentioned that you are looking to grow your business by 20 percent next year. I have a similar focus on growing my business as well. I come across a lot of opportunities to refer my clients and the clients of colleagues to have their carpets cleaned (insert the appropriate business). Would you be able to reciprocate referrals to me as well?"

The opportunity to help other businesspeople grow their businesses will have a synergistic effect. Not every contact will be fruitful; in fact, many will not be, but when you do create a strong connection, it will likely end up being like dynamite and blow the roof off your business (in a good way). As the saying goes, good people know good people, so who knows when that one connection could branch out to several excellent referral connections?

Have about 150 more of those meetings over the next year, and you will build a solid strategic-alliance business pipeline, not to mention that you will build a network of vetted and trusted service providers that you can share with your clients.

Co-Marketing, Credibility, and Opportunities

Once you have established some solid business-to-business referral relationships, it is time to consider leveraging them for maximum effect. One of the best ways to leverage a win-win scenario is to co-market with your referral partner. Whether you have a large marketing operation and budget or you are limited to nearly no budget at all, there are still ways to co-market with little or not cost. For example, if you have a website, offer to list your top and most trusted strategic-alliance partners as "preferred partners" or "exclusive sponsors" on the sponsor and provider page. If you don't have those yet, add them to your website or social media.

Another simple co-marketing tactic is to email out a quick video to your clients offering an exclusive seasonal deal or special rate. If you are working with a heating and air conditioning company, for instance, perhaps its business is slow during seasonal transition times in the late summer or early fall or in the late winter and early spring and could use a boost in business to fill that gap. Your co-marketing efforts position you as a top real estate professional who is connected and also positions your heating and air conditioning partner to fill up its schedule during traditionally slower business months.

Perhaps your carpet cleaning strategic-referral partner is slow in January and February, like most carpet cleaners are. It might include you in its advertising to offer a full market analysis, including a full walk-through to give folks an accurate market value of their home, and if they are considering a move, this is a perfect, no-pressure opportunity to understand the market and how their home compares to others in the area.

The magic of co-marketing provides immediate, built-in trust that comes from a referral from a trusted business source they are familiar with. Your referral partners have standards that their clients already admire, and by aligning with them, they expect you will have similar standards as well. Another aspect is that strategic partnerships can allow you to grow your database exponentially. When you co-market, you are not spamming people or hitting them with junk mail or wasted efforts. They already have a business relationship with one of your strategic partners, so by co-marketing, their clients have an opportunity to become your clients too.

One of the other benefits of co-marketing with strategic alliance partners is that it will showcase you and your real estate practice as connected within the community and position you as the market expert who seems to know everybody.

I am going to pivot briefly and discuss a cold, hard truth. Sometimes strategic-alliance partners slip and stop providing top-shelf service to your clients. Let me be clear; you must never tolerate less than A++ treatment of the people you refer to your partners, period. First off, you are guilty by association. Regardless of the great level of service you provide, you are tied to the level of service that a partner provides to a client that you refer. Never forget how hard you had to work to earn the *privilege* to serve your people. It is a relationship built on trust that can and will be eroded by a poor-quality referral partner. One of the strategies that top real estate agents employ is to "set the stage" upfront with your clients when it comes to referrals by asking clients to let you know if there are any problems with someone or some business that you referred to them. This technique gives you an early warning if a pattern of poor service develops with any of your referral partners.

Be the Connection Hub for People and the Community at Large

Top real estate agents seize the opportunity to serve all people in their community and to position themselves as a *giver*, the foundation they continually build their business on. Top agents understand that to be successful they must build a strategic-alliance network, and that by taking it a step (or six) further, their network can be developed as a trusted resource of service providers, connecting people with people for the greater good. As well, it will make your phone ring. When you are perceived as the connected community expert who seems to know everybody, people will seek you out. People will refer you as a referral source, and people will put you at the top of their list as a top real estate agent. Oddly enough, by positioning yourself as the community expert and the connection maker, you will be forced to explore obscure connection requests. Earlier I mentioned that I once had a client who was in need of an equine trainer, but that request is far from the most obscure. I have had request for acupuncturists, hypnotists, water dousers, and a magician. When somebody asks for an obscure, bizarre, or out-of-left-field referral, you are presented with the possible opportunity to help a magician sell his home and make another one appear!

Members of an Exclusive Clubs

Few things are truer than the fact that there is value in scarcity, meaning that the less available something is, usually the more value that thing has. Knowing that fact, it makes sense that exclusive clubs are no different in that if something is available to "everyone," then it is less valuable than something that is exclusive. There is an element of perceived value here, but for the most part, this adage holds true in most situations. Why not leverage your strategic alliances in such a way that you can offer exclusive "members only" offers to the people in your connected network or sphere? You could focus on past clients, future clients, people who have visited your website, or whomever you might consider worthy of being a member of your club of people who receive offers, discounts, opportunities, and early access to valuable items, events, services, or discounts that are exclusive to your program.

Earlier in this chapter we briefly touched on the idea of designing special offers for your clients from a strategic partner that will be mutually beneficial to your strategic partner as well as your people, such as an early fall furnace service discount or a special rate on an early spring air conditioning tune-up. Top agents know that creating special offers that are exclusively linked to their strategic partner network is ultra-valuable to the public, but when it is an offer that only people who are "in the club" are eligible for, it takes the experience to the next level. In putting together these offers and programs, you can position them as an annual offer that you "train" your clients to expect. By doing this, you will position yourself as the top-of-mind, go-to agent who continues to provide benefits long before or after any transaction occurs. It proves that you are in it for the long haul, you are there to serve your clients, and you are the top resource for all things real estate related and beyond.

One smart way to structure any program that you might implement is to create an opt-in mechanism that requires a login, password, or some sort of gatekeeper system that adds to the exclusiveness of the program. There are companies and printers out there that will print hard cards (similar to grocery store member cards) branded with your logo so that you can arrange discounts for your clients with businesses in your area that you have developed a strategic alliance with.

Perhaps you could arrange special partnership events around clearance sales, retail events, or off-hour dining experiences that are available only to member of your elite members club. We have just scratched the surface on this marketing approach, but the bounds are only as big or small as your creativity. Value, scarcity, and exclusivity are all the makings of a win-win program for your business, the business of your partners, and most of all, the people, clients, and entire network you serve.

Not Just Any Partner Is Worthy of Access to Your Network

For strategic partnerships to work, top agents know that they should be in business partnerships with only businessowners they can rely on to serve clients at the highest levels and with the utmost skill and care, like you do. Without this trust, you may be placing your most precious jewels (your clients) into the hands of careless, reckless, and incompetent hands. With one bad partnership or alliance, the trust of your clients and people network that took months and years to earn could be lost in an instant, never to be regained. Now these are among the worst-case scenarios, but they do occur. Are you willing to gamble on the good standing and solid brand that you took years to develop? Top agents would never do that. Think of the vetting process to be like the interviewing process to make a new hire. The idea that has held steady through time is that of "hire slow and fire fast." Be sure to take the time necessary to ensure that you will be aligning your business with other businesses that are worthy of being trusted to take care of your clients at the highest level. That is not to say that there should be a zero-tolerance policy for mistakes, but strategic partners who fall short or drop the ball with your clients should be held accountable. Second chances should always be earned.

Remember this: your strategic partner did not develop your program, *you did*. Your strategic partners did not come to you with a great program with access to a vast network database that you built; *you came to them*. Never forget that your strategic partners will need you way more than you need them. And the more well-thought-out, elite customer exclusive whiz-bang program you put together, the more value it offers all around, to your clients, your people, and your strategic partners too.

So far in this chapter we have discussed the ins and outs of strategic partnerships and much of how those relationships can be established, fostered, grown, and positioned to flourish and bear fruit for years and years to come with win-win scenarios galore. Now we must focus in on the other side of the same coin: force multipliers.

Force Multipliers Are Game Changers

What makes a force multiplier different from a strategic alliance with a partnering business or service provider? My definition is simple: strategic alliances introduce a third party into the relationship that exists between you and your clients and people network, whereas a force multipliers involve an event, happening, or occurrence designed and executed to benefit your clients and people network and takes place at a specific time and in a specific location for a predetermined audience of your people network and past-client sphere. The preparation is the same whether one of your past clients attends or one thousand. The force multiplier exists in the fact that you can design an event, video, branded gift, seminar, information sharing, or open house with a set level of effort and you can leverage it to be distributed, presented, mailed, or electronically shared with hundreds or even thousands (millions?) of people within your people network, past clients, community, and *the world*. Okay, maybe I am getting a bit carried away again. In the terms of events, they can be reduced to three types: small group events for unique, personal experiences; large group events for exclusive, fun, and entertaining experiences; and seasonal or annual events that build and build over time and can take on a life of their own.

Small group events are great to allow for a more personal connection with people. For instance, you might hire a chef to conduct a hands-on cooking event at your home and choose to invite perhaps seven to ten of your best referral partners and their spouses, guest, or a plus one. These events are best suited for the people who consistently send you referral business or that may have the potential to consistently send you business. These types of events are a great way not only to say thank you with an awesome meal and entertaining evening learning the kitchen secrets of a chef, but also to allow you to connect and cement relationships in a way that is unique and intimate and impactful. These events should be reserved for your most loyal and significant referral partners. These events are typically expensive to host but will provide an intimate setting where you can show appreciation to your most loyal referral partners and best clients.

Large group events are awesome as well. A client appreciation event where you rent out an entire movie theater and invite your past clients and guests to the screening of a new-release movie or an old classic—perhaps a private screening of *National Lampoon's Christmas Vacation* during the holiday season—are great events to host. Another idea is to buy a block of tickets to a major league sporting event and make an afternoon of it. These gatherings are a great way to say thank you to your past clients and people network with an exclusive event that is fun and memorable. There is not as much opportunity to reconnect on an in-depth level, but the opportunity to mingle and make a face-to-face contact with a large number of your past clients and people in your network is invaluable. Within a thirty- to sixty-minute period prior to the movie screening or big game, you could serve hotdogs, say hi, and personally connect with a few hundred people in your network and remind them you are still around and thinking of them. You could also have the opportunity to meet new people, if you allow each family unit or group you invite to bring along a neighbor.

By hosting seasonal or annual events, you can create memorable experiences in a time frame that your clients anticipate and look forward to each year, season, or whatever interval you choose. These types of events are different from the large events, in that they usually take place over a longer period of time. For example, you could host an annual fall festival and hayride with refreshments, food, live music, a costume contest, and picture booth, along with a tractor and hay wagon for hayrides and spooky stories. These events can be structured to last an entire day, with the opportunity for people to come and go all day. Perhaps those with younger children might choose to attend earlier, and others might attend in the evening. The extended timeframe events that take place over an entire day present the opportunity to just say hi and briefly catch up or to have longer conversations and reconnect. You will have opportunities to discuss things with people and past clients that you may not otherwise have the opportunity to visit with very often. These events can be as costly or as inexpensive as you decide. They can be scaled to fit your budget of time, money, and resources accordingly. The truth is that events are an excellent force multiplier.

Another great force multiplier is through the use of video. In today's world where everybody walks around with a mini television screen in their hands, what better way to connect than through well executed videos? First, people are busy, so video is an on-demand, nonintrusive, interesting, and captivating form of communication. Video communication also gives you the ability to get your message and information to your audience using both verbal and nonverbal communication, which can convey messages with emotion and in an impactful way. Most of all, video allows you to be scripted, articulate, and fun. The basic video production capabilities available on most of our operating systems today have the ability to make us all into Steven Spielberg with a fifteen- to thirty-minute investment of our time and effort.

Another more traditional example of a force multiplier is the occasional tchotchke (pronounced chach-KEE). A tchotchke, an old Yiddish term, is a knickknack or trinket, a simple, small item of high perceived value, usually branded, that is sent out on a consistent schedule (quarterly, bi-annually, yearly), usually via postal mail, along with a clever note or message. To be effective, the tchotchke must have a few important characteristics. One, it must remind the receiver of you and what you do. The best approach top agents take is to give an item designed to be used frequently within the household. Second, the item should be universally useful and have a long shelf life, for instance a flyswatter in the shape of a house with your logo on it. And finally, it must be planned and budgeted accordingly, in order to be highly affective. Some traditional examples are refrigerator magnets, flyswatters, notepads, ink pens, sewing kits, bottle openers, pot and pan scrapers, or a ruler. Many items fit the criteria. The only limitations are your imagination and your budget. A word to the wise, this force multiplier is effective, but it is expensive and can run upward of one to four dollars or more per mailing. In my experience, it usually works out that the less expensive the item is, the less effective the force multiplier is. Top agents understand that it takes a hefty budget to do the tchotchke right, not always, but almost always, so know what you are getting into before you risk your time and treasure.

Essentials of Consistent Communication

The items that fall into the consistent and routine communication category of force multipliers are emails and postal mailers that contain market information, community information, homeowner information, or proof of performance information. Most of these items are self-explanatory; however, in the case of proof of performance information, I will elaborate.

Proof of performance information can be summed up into one simple idea: bragging material, the tried-and-true "look what I sold and look how much I sold it for and look how fast I sold it" type of mailer. Some of the rules of the road on these types of communication are to become very predictable as to when you will send them, such as once a quarter, or maybe three times each year. For example, January, May, and October is a great schedule, but make it a regularly scheduled and executed program. Also, it must be useful information that is short, sweet, and easy to understand at a quick glance. You will miss the mark by trying to cram in too much information. It is important to make the point to not overdo the bragging in your brag pieces. People will generally tolerate a bit of bragging from a humble servant, but be careful not to go over the top and position yourself as an extreme braggadocio.

Educational Seminars Are a Great Way to Connect

When real estate agents think of the word *seminar* it usually conjures up thoughts of the usual First Time Buyer Seminar or the Real Estate Investment Seminar. I will say that when structured properly and executed at a high level, both these types of seminars can be highly valuable and successful at both presenting useful information and generating high quality business. However, you can present information on interesting and timely topics other than the hard-core real estate sales format. Top agents realize when it comes to putting together a one- or two-hour seminar containing compelling, interesting, and useful subject matter, the only limitation is the creativity of the agent. Consider subjects such as "You're ten years out from retirement; what should you know that might cost you big," where you assemble a panel of three or four experts in the areas of finance, Social Security benefits, investments, and tax codes. This type of seminar can present a wealth of valuable information that is very useful for people ten years or fewer from retirement. As well, this group within your past clients and network of people are likely empty nesters who may be looking to downsize or want to leverage the equity in their home to create passive rental income. The key is always to make use of the credibility and expertise of third-party presenters from other fields, such as insurance, investing, or estate planning. Be sure that you know who you are dealing with, and do not align yourself with shysters, one-and-done artists, slick willies, and leg-humpers—you can imagine the types. Always be on the hunt for true professionals. Perhaps your strategic alliances are full of true professionals and you have your pick of the litter. If not, it is time to focus on building your partner network and strategic alliances. Two birds, one stone; you get the picture.

When you do choose to go full-on "real estate silverback gorilla" and hold a hard-core real estate seminar to discuss buying, selling, or investing in real estate, you must think creatively and pack a punch when it comes to providing great information. Get creative with the title. Rather than First Time Buyer Seminar, use more flash with a title like Seven Things to Avoid That Could Cost You Thousands of Dollars When Buying Your First Home.

As well, make sure that you have a few experts on hand such as a home inspector, appraiser, lender, title or escrow officer, or countless other experts involved in various aspects of the home-buying process. Always issue some form of ticket or registration to attendees. It allows you to track the interest and attendance levels in advance so you can adjust the size of the room, gauge the amount of refreshments needed, and capture basic contact information, so you can touch base with them and confirm their attendance prior to the event.

Open Houses Are the Biggest and Best Force Multiplier

Surprise! In case you did not already know, the biggest and best opportunity to enlist the power of a force multiplier to build your real estate sales business is by holding open-house events. Think about it; the script writes itself. Top agents know that open house events are, without a doubt, the number-one way to showcase their high-level value proposition. First of all, let's take a moment to establish the primary focus of top agents when holding an open house. Any guesses? I will give you two big hints; it is *not* to find buyers, and it is *not* to sell the house you are holding open. Those scenarios do play out, but not often. I find in my market that about one out of every 150 individuals that walk through an open house will actually have an interest in writing an offer on the house. As well, about one out of every thirty individuals that walk through an open house will *not* be represented by an agent and *is* in the legitimate need of an agent. By far there are much better odds of finding a buyer to serve when holding an open house event than the odds of actually selling the home, but statistically speaking, for about every three open-house events you hold, you will find a legitimate buyer that needs representation of an agent. If you are not positioning yourself to secure more listings when holding open house events, then you are approaching it with the wrong mindset.

First, an open-house event presents you with limitless low-cost and no-cost opportunities to interact with people and discuss real estate. Depending on the restrictions in your particular area, there are opportunities to knock on fifty to one hundred or more doors in the neighborhood promoting your open-house event. There are opportunities to distribute fliers or mailers to area homeowners about the upcoming event. You can promote it with online ads and targeted social media posts. You can associate your face with the neighborhood, and countless other ideas, because open-house events are your opportunity to get creative. Top agents know that their ultimate focus when holding open-house events is to showcase their strong work ethic and creative marketing abilities to all the surrounding homeowners. Perhaps invite the neighbors for an exclusive first look and an opportunity to "pick your new neighbor," if in fact they see the home and think they may know someone who is in the market to live in the neighborhood. Open-house events present the opportunity to leverage your network of strategic alliance partners, such as lenders and home insurance experts, to answer on-the-spot questions about the house. The opportunities to showcase your many talents as a real estate agent are limited only by your thinking.

One sidenote for agents who may not currently have a listing to hold an open-house event: fear not. All is not lost. All you have to do is find another agent who is willing to allow you to hold an open-house event at one of his or her current listings. It does take some time to prospect for agents in your brokerage or in another brokerage who might allow you to hold their client's listing open, but in a short time you will likely build a network of four or five agents who will become reliable sources of listings where you can hold events. One little trick that I developed early on in my real estate career was to offer to provide the listing agent with a detailed report outlining all the important details that occurred during the open-house event. Some of the items I listed were the weather conditions, drive-by traffic count, feedback on the property, number of parties who visited, and a marketing summary, just to name a few. I explained to the listing agent that I would be listed on the report as the agent on sight; however, I would put the agents' logos and pictures on the top and present them as the "hero" to their clients, basically letting them take credit for all my hard work. It was a win-win; they looked to be great, hard-working agents in the eyes of their client, and I was able to make contact with the rest of the neighborhood and showcase my talents. I will tell you that this open house event strategy was, by far, the most effective method I used to launch my career in real estate sales.

How far are you willing to go to hyper-leverage force multipliers and strategic alliances to take your real estate sales career to stratospheric levels?

11

Their Real Estate Advisor for Life

The distinction of being a real estate advisor is easily summed up in one sentence: Real estate advisors are top real estate agents who, by nature, have a big-picture mindset in their overall approach to business and work hard to provide value and build long-term relationships with the clients they serve.

Agents who approach the real estate business with the singular focus of completing the transaction, collecting a commission check, and moving on to the next transaction are not focused on building long-term relationships. All sales are final in their eyes, and each client represents a service rendered and a payment collected with little thought of the future. Do not misunderstand me; some transactional agents are very good at the craft of real estate sales and deliver a high-quality representation on each transaction they complete. However, very rarely will they go the extra mile, and rarely do they approach their clients with aspirations to serve their long-term best interests.

A top real estate agent who serves as an advisor, however, seeks out and shares information and advises clients of their options, both in the here and now and in the long term. An advisor is similar to a watch dog, constantly vigilant and aware of the best interests of their clients, to whom they will be loyal and protect as long as they are standing guard.

Whether or not people are aware, everybody needs a real estate advisor. The mindset with many in the public is that they will just "use" an agent to get the job done and then move on. Sadly, this thinking is a result of years of agents using clients to collect a commission check after the transaction and then moving on.

Let's not forget that in almost every case, the buying or selling of a home is typically the largest single transaction that a person will undertake in a lifetime. That statistic is something that is thrown around quite often in the real estate business, and for good reason. However, it is often overlooked that most of the average homeowner's net worth and most of their wealth is tied up in their home. Not in every case, but for a large number of homeowners in this country, their home is their single largest collection of wealth. It is clear that anyone with a real estate license could sell a home for a client, but enlisting the long-term service of a true real estate advisor is one of the wisest things that homeowners can do to help guide their decisions and protect their largest single store of wealth. It really is a no-brainer. Unfortunately, though, most homeowners do not experience that level of service from the real estate agents they work with. As well, it is important to recognize that people's homes are more than just a primary residence these days. For most homeowners their home is also an office or a nursery or the overall heart of their family, where many important aspects of their lives take place. People need and deserve an advisor on their side focused on their long-term goals and the goals and desires of their families. The problem is that many homeowners never experience the high level of service that top real estate agents provide and are probably unaware that there actually are agents who provide this level of service. It is our job to seek out opportunities to put on our red capes with the purpose of saving clients from weak experiences with weak agents. As top real estate agents know, educating the public on such matters is just another line item in a long list of obligations that they have to the public that they interact with daily.

Serving as an Advisor Requires a Long-Term Mindset

If you think back to the discussions around earning the loyalty of a client in chapter four, you will remember that it takes a significant amount of reinforcement and repetition to build business relationships rooted in loyalty and trust. And it all starts with the agent. Rome was not built in a day, and in the same line of reasoning, relationships foundationally built on loyalty and trust are earned over time. In fact, they are usually earned over significant time. Consider that the average amount of time that homeowners in America stay in their home is between seven and ten years, so the buying and selling cycles are not an everyday occurrence for homeowners. This single bit of information illustrates the importance of focusing on serving clients with a long-term mindset of a real estate advisor.

To serve a client at the highest level, a real estate advisor must always be aware of the entirety of the big picture of a client's situation. As a comparison, consider the role of major league baseball pitchers who are closers. They do not enter the game cold, with no idea of the situation, such as how many outs there are, who the next batters in the lineup are, and most of all, the score of the game. Closers do not just take a nap until they are called up in the middle of the ninth inning, completely oblivious to the game situation they are facing. A typical major league baseball game usually takes three or more hours from start to finish. A closer may be on the field for sometimes one pitch, one out, or one inning. Closers may be out on the field for only a few minutes, but they were at the game the whole time, following the cadence of the game, watching and waiting for the time when the team needs their specialized skills. When that time comes, they are ready to take the field, completely aware of the score of the game and what is at stake.

In the same vein, top real estate agents know that even though they may be on the field, so to speak, for only a few months of the nearly ten years clients own their home, they must know what is at stake and they have to be acutely aware of the score of the game that the client is playing. This is the foundation of being a client's real estate advisor for life.

A real estate advisor must know clients' bigger picture when it comes to their wants, needs, and goals. As real estate professionals we stay in tune with ever-changing market conditions, momentum shifts in the market, and long- and short-term trends. When we understand the bigger picture of our clients, we can present our clients with opportunities that fit their situation as well as identifying some rare opportunities that may be of immense benefit to their bottom line. By taking the approach of a real estate advisor, you can literally connect the dots of market conditions that your clients may not be in the position to see. After all, an advisor in the realm of real estate is like the guard dog standing watch, one who will remain alert and bring attention to any big threat (or opportunity) as it relates to their clients.

Annual Real Estate Reviews with Clients

Just like most things in the business of real estate sales, the right thing is easy to do; unfortunately it is also easy *not* to do. It was drilled into my head from early on in my real estate career that if something is not scheduled in writing on your calendar, it simply does not exist. Simplified, if a person is not purposeful in clearly scheduling an event and defining when, where, and how long it will take place, it will most likely not happen. The annual real estate review is at the top of the list of good intentions that easily fall by the wayside. If something is a priority, scheduled on your calendar, it will happen; otherwise it will not happen. Top agents know that interactions with their clients such as annual real estate reviews form the bedrock of a solid business relationship where they position themselves as a real estate advisor of life. Considering that people move on average every seven to ten years, an annual real estate review presents the opportunity to stay informed on changes in your clients' plans as a result of changes in family size, job changes, or developments in the neighborhood. There is nothing better to cement a long-term relationship with your clients than being face to face with your clients and having a fifteen- to thirty-minute high-level discussion about one of their largest stores of wealth. The annual real estate review will keep both you and your clients on the same page and in sync with the general state of affairs that will most affect the bigger picture when it comes to the planning and timing of their next move. It is a fact of life that markets change, neighborhoods change, and even cities change. Maybe a new apartment complex is being built near a client's home that may impact traffic patterns in the future or a road expansion will bring much needed relief to traffic congestion or a school has been approved to be built. Any number of things could directly impact the sale of a home in a given area, and an annual review is the opportunity where those things can be discussed, anticipated, and planned for, as they may relate to the timing of a move. Top agents understand that without an annual real estate review, or at the very least, without sharing a simple comparative market analysis with each of your clients annually, they are nothing more than short-sighted agents out there chasing commissions.

Clients and Their Home Improvement Projects

As real estate agents, we know which home improvement projects add to the value of a home and which just do not. As with most financial matters, people are seeking to maximize their return on investment, or they at least would like to know up front what the likely return on the money and time they spend on a home improvement project might be. Even if the project they are planning is likely to bring zero return on investment, it is always better to know up front. As well, not every project is focused on creating a return on investment. I once received a request from homeowners asking what their home might sell for in the current market, so I conducted a market analysis. Upon visiting the home, I discovered that it had many expensive upgrades in the basement that would likely bring no return on investment. The clients had a child in his early twenties who was tragically injured in an accident and was paralyzed from the chest down. To help their twenty-something adjust to the new lifestyle he was facing, they converted their entire basement into a functioning living space that would accommodate the day-to-day rigors of living with paralysis. The young adult had been planning to move to New York City prior to the accident, so in making the basement improvements, the parents chose a unique city-themed design for the project. In advising them, I explained that the basement was perfectly suited to their unique circumstances, but it was not going to bring them much in the way of added equity in the home. Most likely the basement would have to be converted back to a more traditional living space, or they would actually trade some equity to cover the cost of a future buyer having to make the conversion. In this case, the clients were not happy with my assessment and did not understand why all of the nearly $80,000 investment they had made, which at the time was more than one-fifth of the home's value, was not going to be recaptured. The truth of the matter was that the basement was so specialized that it had only one function: accommodating a paraplegic person in his twenties who loved New York City. In spite of my detailed explanations and examples, they disagreed with my assessment and chose to list with another agent. A few weeks later when the house was listed in the MLS, I noticed that the agent listed the home at the same price the sellers had wanted me to list the house for. The home sat and sat on the market for months and months and finally ended up selling for less than what I had originally proposed. I was not involved when they made the decision to convert the basement for their paralyzed child. I suspect that if I had been involved, and if I had the opportunity to explain all of this information to them upfront, they probably still would have decided to make the improvements. It was clear that they loved their kid and that their focus was making life the best they could for him after sustaining such a devastating and life-altering injury. The only difference may have been that they would have understood the total costs of making those unique, one-off improvements to their home, and perhaps they would have been better prepared with a plan when it came time to sell. I know that if I were involved from the beginning as their advisor, I could have helped make the situation better.

Another reason top real estate agents encourage their clients to discuss home improvement projects with them is that most agents have a network of vetted professionals in their strategic alliance. In most cases, an agent may have worked out a discount or added services that might not be available to those outside of their strategic alliance network. One more obvious reason is that perhaps the proposed home improvement does not make financial sense in terms of time and money, and the better choice would be to sell the current home and purchase another home that already has the desired improvements. As a real estate advisor, you can provide an expanded view of the entire situation and help clients avoid tunnel vision that occurs when people get so fixated on solving a problem that they may not realize they are actually causing a few more problems than they are actually solving.

Bottom line, in conducting yourself as clients' real estate advisor for life, you will be the first person they think of when they think of real estate. Throughout my career it has never ceased to amaze me how my clients associate all things related to a house with me. It is more than you might ever imagine. I believe they do it because I constantly position myself in their "line of sight" when it comes to assisting them with all things real estate related.

Ask yourself this question: how do you think clients will respond to some agent they run into at an open house, an agent who sends them marking materials, or an agent who holds an open house in their neighborhood? I know the answer, because my clients have told me. They say these seven beautiful words: "I am already working with an agent."

The truth of the matter is that I was there, I was part of their real estate life, long before any Johnny-come-lately agent out pounding the pavement on the hunt for their next client. It is a proven fact that when you show up for your clients in a big way, they will be loyal to you. Hey, you know, maybe that would be a great premise on which to structure the foundation of a real estate business. Pardon me; I am just thinking out loud.

How Agents Use a First-Year System Effectively

When I refer to a first-year system or a year-one system, I am referring to the first-year marketing plan that you use after your clients purchase a home. The idea behind putting in place a first-year system is to start the post-sale relationship off on the right foot, proving that they are your clients for life and not a cheap one-time deal. These programs can be designed in endless ways and configured to accommodate virtually all styles of agents and their unique ways of conducting business and communicating with past clients. The key to designing a successful system is to make several contacts in the first three months of the process. This is the time when your clients are most happy and most likely to talk with friends and family about their home purchase experience and when they will be enthusiastically referring you to the people they know. Another key element to consider when structuring any type of first-year program is that the program should be rooted in gratitude. Clients should know how important they are to you and the continued success of your real estate business. They should know how much you value them, and the only way is to show them by purposeful, systematic, and meaningful communication. Top agents put in this type of hard work daily to bring never-ending value to their clients, because they know that continuing and growing their relationship with their clients is the ultimate show of gratitude. I believe that most agents are not out just chasing commissions, and obviously our clients represent much more to us than just a paycheck, but are clients aware of that fact? Do your actions prove that information to them clearly, concisely, and without question? By being present long after closing, you will be there to assist them in ways they are not even aware of, such as with your strategic network, by sharing community information, or simply by providing them with an annual update on the market value of their home. As I have said many times, it is our jobs as agents to be loyal to our clients, and through those efforts, we will earn their loyalty and trust.

Also, continuing to stay in contact with clients after closing lengthens the shelf life of their appreciation of your hard work. This is particularly helpful in situations where the transaction might have had some challenges or turbulence. Even if you brought the transaction in for a safe and successful landing, do not underestimate the power of mending the memories of any rough patches with a strong and well-designed first-year system. By nature we humans want to leave bad experiences in the past and forget them. Top agents know that a first-year program is a powerful tool to show clients how much they care about them, especially if things did not go as smoothly as anticipated. The first three months after closing are the perfect time to mend fences and show your clients what you are all about when it comes to customer service.

One of the critical things you can ask for from clients after a transaction closes is for their opinion on what you did well and where you could improve. One of the best ways to gather this information is with an anonymous survey. The survey does not have to be super in depth and overly complex. It can comprise as few as three to five questions. People are more honest and willing to share criticism and suggestions for improvement if they believe the survey is anonymous and not linked to them or their name. Some of the easiest ways to conduct these surveys is to have a colleague send it on your behalf or perhaps it can be sent and collected by an administrator within your brokerage. Online survey companies are also a good resource. Valuable feedback is best collected when the transaction is fresh in the client's mind and easily recalled.

The Value of a Strong Referral Agent Network

Most brokerages today have a solid digital infrastructure when it comes to their agents being able to pass referrals and network with agents outside of their primary market areas. With most national brokerages, these databases are usually included in your basic interface or portal connected to the national or regional brokerage. As well, most brokerages have annual events that agents attend, and many will travel from all over the region or country to attend, depending on the size of the brokerage where you hang your license. It is our mission to protect and serve our clients, and if we can get them in contact with an agent from another part of the country when they are being relocated or buying a vacation property, then we should do it. Remember, trust is transferrable, and you can easily vet agents with a quick review of their production numbers and a phone call. And do not forget, you also get a reward for successfully connecting your clients with top-quality agents in other markets in the form of a referral fee, if the other agent agrees to pay one, which they typically will do. Win-win situations are the best, and agent referrals definitely fall into that category.

Some of the other activities that top agents perform to position themselves as professional-level real estate advisors is by proactively interpreting and dissecting the current real estate "buzz." Much of the real estate information that floats around today on the internet or the evening news is easily misinterpreted or oversimplified, and what is going on in one market may be the exact opposite of the market conditions taking place in a nearby city or town. Whether the information pertains to price point fluctuations, multiple offer situations, inventory pressures, or just some zesty market value estimates that are completely full of hot air, your professional analysis is extremely valuable to your network of people. Perhaps you share this information by blogging, sending video updates, or in your monthly newsletter. However you choose to provide this information, people will always be interested in what is going on in the real estate market and will be glad to receive your timely updates. If you do not believe me, just mention that you are a real estate agent at the next cocktail party you attend and see what happens.

As we discussed in the last chapter, creating a club and sharing exclusive offers and events with your clients is not only a great force multiplier but also a great way to add value and position you as a real estate advisor for life. Some of the other added benefits to the people in your network are that you will, by nature of the events you organize and hold, connect people who might otherwise not have connected. Not only are you serving as a connection hub when it comes to valued vendors, service providers, and contractors, you are also a potential connector of people. Who knows what types of business partnerships may form or love connection may bloom? When you are the connection hub of your network, without a doubt, there are no limits.

One of the most important functions in positioning yourself as a real estate advisor for life is that you are able to serve as a barrier between your people and the bozos out there. First off, the bozos are dangerous and create messes that you may end up being asked to fix, and most of the time you will be fixing them for free. If someone in a weak moment hires a weak agent, it can turn out to be a full-blown mess. Do not allow that to happen. Show your value and prevent those situations from arising in the first place.

Serve a Purpose Bigger than Real Estate

Earlier in this chapter I said that a person's home is so much more than just four walls and a roof. People's homes touch nearly every aspect of their lives. Homes are where memories are made, lives are shared, children grow, loved ones pass on. Homes are full of all of those in-between moments that blossom into the human experience.

We have the opportunity to develop and use our real estate superpowers to bring much joy and good to the world. A career in real estate is a noble undertaking, and if you choose to see it for what it is and what it could be, you will literally be able to change people's lives for the better. A life worth living is one in which we focus on filling the cups of the others around us, and when we live our lives that way, through our real estate business and beyond, our cup will truly runneth over.

www.ingramcontent.com/pod-product-compliance
Lightning Source LLC
Chambersburg PA
CBHW050110210326
41519CB00015BA/3906